It's never too late ...

A practical guide to continuing education for women of all ages

Joan Perkin

i
impact books

This edition published in Great Britain in 1993 by
Impact Books Limited
151 Dulwich Road, London SE24 0NG

© Joan Perkin 1984, 1993

All rights reserved. No part of this publication may
be reproduced in any form or by any means without
the prior permission of Impact Books Ltd.

ISBN   1 874687 20 X

For my family:
Harold, Deborah and Julian –
with thanks for their loving
help and support.
Joan Perkin

Cover illustration by Nicky Dupays

Typeset by
Paperweight Print Production & Design Consultants, London SE24
Printed and bound by The Guernsey Press, Guernsey

Contents

Introduction vii

Chapter 1 **Making a fresh start – why not you?** 1

Chapter 2 **Believing in yourself** 7
Don't feel guilty 7
Recognize the skills you have 12

Chapter 3 **Choosing a course** 17
Where to begin 17
Making contact with a college 18
Return-to-work courses 20
Return-to-study courses 25
GCSE and A level courses 26
Alternatives to A levels 29
Diploma of Higher Education courses 30
Courses at adult residential colleges 31
Teacher training 33

Chapter 4 **Aiming for a degree** 35
Universities 37
Colleges and Institutes of Higher Education 50
The Open University (OU) 53
London University External Degree Scheme 60
Checklist 61

Chapter 5 **Finding the money** 63
What do you need money for? 63
Who gets money for study? 63
Where do you apply for a grant? 64
For which courses are grants available? 67
Grants from LEAs 68
How are LEA grants paid? 74
Other financial concessions and entitlements 76

What is the easiest way to get money to study? 78

Chapter 6 **Fitting in at college 81**
Will you feel out of place? 81
Life after class 85

Chapter 7 **Getting down to study 93**
A good place to study 94
Learn to take, keep and use good notes 96
Learn to read rapidly and with understanding 100
Learn to present reports concisely 103
Learn to write essays 104

Chapter 8 **Getting the family on your side 109**
Does your partner understand you? 109
Becoming a student can benefit your marriage 112
Student mothers are better mothers 115

Chapter 9 **Caring for the children 121**
Care for the under fives 122
Care for the over fives 132

Chapter 10 **Sharing the housework 137**
Organize 138
Finding time for study 139

Chapter 11 **Looking ahead – applying for jobs 149**
Sources of careers advice 149
Hunting for jobs 150
Job applications 152
Interviews 154
Possible snags 156
Think positively 157

Chapter 12 **People like you 159**

Conclusion 177

Introduction

Who is this book for?
This book is for women of all ages who have missed out on further education earlier in their lives, whatever the reason, and who are interested in making up for lost opportunities.

There are millions of talented women in Britain who could successfully take education and training courses and transform their lives. It might require some reordering of their activities, but it would certainly be enjoyable and worthwhile.

Why is the book specifically for women?
Returning to study is difficult for anyone, but women have special problems and need more help to find their way into the maze of continuing education:

1. Old-fashioned prejudice There is still a belief that education is wasted on women, because they just get married, have babies and stay at home. But the days of the traditional family are well and truly over; few families now expect the man to be the sole bread-winner for the rest of his life; women want and expect to work outside the home for all or part of their lives. Yet women themselves still accept the judgement that it is less important for a woman to be educated than for a man.

Clearly, women need to be given greater encouragement to return to education than men who are traditionally expected to take initiatives to satisfy their ambitions and provide for their dependants.

And women have to find the confidence to believe in their own abilities.

2. The image of educated women Too many people still hold an out-of-date view that educated women tend to be aggressive and unfeminine. High achievers of either sex *may* be aggressive, but quiet confidence in personal ability is an equally successful tactic. Education will not necessarily change your personality, but it should give you the confidence to come forward and accept more responsibility.

3. The domestic burden Women still tend to take the major responsibility for domestic matters though it is becoming more common for husbands to accept that they have *some* responsibility for household chores and looking after children. All women can plan and share household duties more equitably.

4. Ignorance of opportunities Women frequently don't know what is available by way of education and training.

Why do you need this book now?
At a time of high unemployment (especially for women) do we need more educated women? Yes, *everybody* has a right to education and training beyond school level, if they want it, and it should be available at any time in your life, even if you don't at the moment want or need a job. But you should always study as if you might one day work, for example in the event of financial need, divorce or widowhood, because a woman with education will always have the edge in the job market over women without. Large numbers of women already work outside the home, of course, and for those without formal qualifications education is their best hope of career advancement.

Moreover, Britain is a small, overcrowded island with few resources, and we must live by our brains. Women's brains are not inferior to men's – and men and governments will be very glad about this before the end of the century. We shall need all the educated people – all the people trained to cope with the problems of the world – we can get, and *women are our greatest under-utilized resource*. Again, Britain cannot afford to stand still – there is need for innovation, retraining, second careers and women as well as men may need to change careers or upgrade their skills.

Women of all ages and all classes have a need for self-fulfilment, of making the best of themselves and their opportunities. Men and career women often get it through their jobs.

Women without jobs – or who want a better job – can get it through continuing education. There are hundreds of things you can do.

This book sets out to tempt you into the vast garden of opportunity which is known as higher, further and continuing education. Chapters 1 and 2 suggest ways of building confidence in yourself and your ability to cope with a course of training or education. Chapter 3 looks at some of the many courses available at non-advanced level, whereas Chapter 4 is concerned with ways of choosing a degree course. Chapter 5 looks at ways of finding financial help, and Chapter 6 is concerned with how you could fit in happily at college. Chapter 7 is dealing with study methods. Chapter 8 looks at ways of getting the family on your side when you undertake a college course, and Chapter 9 is concerned with the problems of looking after children when you are a student. Chapter 10 suggests ways of tackling the housework more effectively. Chapter 11 will be of interest to women who want to get a job at the end of their course. Chapter 12 is a series of case-studies, of women who went back to college and succeeded.

The whole book, it is hoped, will be of use to women of any age and any previous level of educational attainment who feel that they can better themselves by returning to study but don't quite know how to go about it. For all of you it has one hopeful message: *it's never too late*.

Chapter 1
Making a fresh start – why not you?

- Are you over the normal student age (18 to 22)?
- Did you miss out on education after leaving school?
- Are you bored with seeing the same faces and hearing the same opinions day after day?
- Would you like to come alive to a world of new ideas?
- Are you fed up with giving tremendous amounts of time and energy to voluntary work, for which you get little or no status or recognition?
- Would you like a paid job outside the home, either now or at some time in the future?
- Have you already got a paid job, but want to change it for another job with more interest and responsibility?
- Are you willing to put a lot of effort into making up for lost opportunities?

If you can answer 'yes' to some of these questions, why not think about becoming a student? It does not necessarily mean taking three years of full-time study – it can be as little as one evening a week at a class plus some home study. And between these two extremes lie a multitude of possibilities, all of them interesting, exciting and full of promise for the future. Before considering the choices and deciding which course suits your needs, it might be helpful to think about some general questions that women contemplating continuing education tend to ask.

Do you have to be a special woman to become a student?
No, women students are a very diverse lot. They vary in age from 18 to over 70. Those over 21 when they begin an undergraduate degree course are technically known as mature students, and they have certain advantages when applying to universities and colleges, which will be discussed later. For grants purposes, however, the minimum age for a mature student is 25, so this can be

confusing. But this book is for mature women in the general sense: women mature enough to know that they are missing something in their lives and to think that education might fill that gap. They include married women living with their husbands; women who are widowed, separated or divorced, single women with or without children; women with six children or more; and women who never want to have children. If you become a mature student, you will find yourself side by side with women of different races, classes and incomes, from widely different home circumstances and backgrounds. Some will be women who have never had a job; others will have given up paid work to study full-time; still others will be working part-time and studying part-time. So it is very difficult to point to any one mature woman student as 'typical' of the rest. Yet they all obviously have one thing in common: they want to learn more, and they are willing to take a leap in the dark by returning to formal education. They are also willing to put a lot of hard work into getting what they want out of life.

Isn't it more difficult for a woman to get a place on an education course?

It shouldn't be, and you must not be defeatist about it. Women are now nearly half the students in universities and colleges, and the majority in part-time adult education courses. Of course, women are still a minority within a minority receiving *higher* education at degree level in colleges and universities, but things are changing, and women are getting a bigger slice of the educational cake. In 1990, 9% of women aged between 25 and 29 had a degree or equivalent qualification, compared with 12% of men (*Social Trends*, HMSO, 1992).

Most colleges and universities want the best students they can get, and because they *are* a minority women are now the biggest reservoir of bright students. It is highly unlikely that you will be turned down because you are a woman, but if you have any difficulty on this score you can get advice from the Equal Opportunities Commission, Overseas House, Quay Street, Manchester M3 3HN.

Will I enjoy college as much as I would have done when I was 18?

Making a fresh start – why not you?

You can't bring back yesterday, however much you would like to, and you can't expect as a mature student to recapture your youth. But you will enjoy it in a different way, and perhaps, with your greater experience of life and work, even more than you would have done at 18. Most 18 to 22 year olds like having older students in their classes, because they bring a greater knowledge of the world outside school and college, and a sharper sense of realism to discussions, especially of history, literature and social studies. You will share with the young feelings about lectures and lecturers, essay writing, the problem of getting hold of library books, and so on. They will probably invite you to some of their discos, parties and drinking sessions, and whether you go and enjoy them depends on the sort of person you are. Some of these activities simply make some people feel old, but you are as young as you feel, and some mature students are the life and soul of the party. The great thing about the young is their enthusiasm and questioning of everything. You will constantly have your ideas challenged, and you may begin to see things from their perspective. For example, most people of my generation were taught to think it a virtue to 'postpone gratification' of immediate desires in favour of long-term benefits that were supposed to follow. But you will find that many young students think it crazy not to enjoy every minute of life as it passes, making the most of opportunities as they arise. And why should we be so sure that their way is worse than ours? Of course in the 1990s, there is a new seriousness among students, both about the world's problems and their own future.

Will I be able to keep up with the rest of my class?
This can seem difficult at first, if you are studying with young people who have had no break in their education. But there is no need to despair, especially if you take a return-to-study class and recognize that basic skills can be acquired with practice. Memory can be improved, and as we get older our conceptual powers increase. And you will soon find you have advantages you little suspected: the young are so often theorizing about things that you know by first-hand experience. You will find them coming to you for advice and information – not all of it academic! Remember, too, that thousands of other women have gone back to college

It's never too late ...

and have come through with flying colours. The failure rate for older students is very small indeed – over 90% of them succeed.

Could I fit in at an 'ivory tower' of learning like a university?
What do you mean by an ivory tower? Do you mean a place far removed from the hurly-burly of everyday life, where intellectuals discuss the meaning of life and how to put the world to rights? Do you think of universities as places full of high-minded individuals who do not struggle for power or resort to petty squabbles? If so, you will be disappointed to find that universities are not centres of sweetness and light, though they certainly house many of the finest brains in the country. You may meet as much prejudice against women in universities as elsewhere, for example. Academics are just ordinary people who happen to have specialized in a particular field of knowledge. What they know, they know thoroughly and professionally, and their job is to make you think not like them but for yourself. They will encourage you to read widely and critically, to re-examine your present ideas, and to develop arguments to sustain your beliefs. You will find plenty of people, both staff and students, willing to spend time discussing unusual ideas, and you may be surprised to find that ideas you thought new have been debated endlessly down the centuries. Kicking ideas around is the fun part of being a student: you don't have to put your ideas into practice, so you can play a sort of intellectual game in which you turn the world upside down and reshape it in any way you please.

If I take a college course, will I be sure to get a good job afterwards, if I want one?
With unemployment at nearly 3 million people, no-one is *sure* to get a job or keep a job nowadays. A lot depends on which course you take, at what level of expertise, and what job you hope to get at the end of it. It is fairly certain that your job prospects will improve if you have definite qualifications. Education and training at any level are likely to open the door to more fulfilling and better-paid work. At the very least, further education will give you an edge over unqualified people in getting whatever job is going. Higher education is a good investment of your time and energy: careers and counselling services report that most graduates find

jobs eventually – even when there is widespread unemployment. According to *Social Trends,* HMSO, 1992, graduates have an easier time getting satisfying jobs than do non-graduates, and most of them get jobs with prospects of advancement. There has been no study of what happens to mature women students in Britain (as far as I know), but a recent study in America showed that three-quarters of 're-entry' (i.e. mature) women students felt that their college courses had been worthwhile because they had expanded their employment opportunities. Less advanced education can give you an edge, too. For example, night classes in book-keeping or technical drawing might mean the difference between a better job and staying in the same old rut.

Education will not guarantee you the particular job you want, but it will give you a fighting chance of getting it. What you will have is the choice of looking for a skilled or professional job. For many women, working outside the home and having a job title and separate income provides a sense of identity, and an intellectual challenge that gives added meaning to life. Being qualified to take a job also provides an insurance against some of the traumatic changes that can happen to any woman – widowhood, being 'dumped' by your husband or partner, wanting to leave your parents or partner, or needing to support a parent or partner who becomes unemployed or an invalid.

If I take an education course and get a grant for it, am I obliged to take a job afterwards?
No. If you receive a government grant to take a course of education, there is no condition attached to it. No-one is going to force you to take a job at the end of it, if you don't want to.

Can I afford to be a student?
If you haven't an income or resources of your own, there is a wide range of student grants and allowances available. Most people on full-time courses get some grant, and their fees are paid. The rules are complex, and you will find more details in Chapter 5 below.

Can education help me cure my middle-aged blues?
If it can't, then nothing else will. Perhaps you have been a full-time mother for some years, and now find yourself feeling useless

It's never too late ...

and depressed because your children are growing up. Or perhaps you are dissatisfied with what you have achieved in your working life so far. You may be looking for ways to live more as an individual (rather than at second-hand through husband, children or parents). In middle life you might find it harder to force yourself to make the decision to come out and look for opportunities to express yourself differently, but once you make up your mind you will find it pays off. Further education will give you confidence to express your own ideas and opinions, and knowledge to back up your arguments, and that is exciting and exhilarating.

Could I manage a course and look after my baby?
You could look around for a college which has a creche or other baby-minding facilities. Failing this, you would need to pay a baby-sitter, find another person with a similar problem and baby-sit for each other in turn, or take a class when your husband or partner can look after the baby. If you want to take a full-time course, you will have to make regular baby-minding arrangements and be sure they are completely satisfactory. This problem is discussed in Chapter 9 below. Few mature students are super organizers, but they all have to learn to organize their lives to some extent. Those who have survived have learned to arrange their lives to suit both themselves and their families, and have made sure they had ample time to study. Some ideas on how to go about this are given in Chapter 10.

How can I find the confidence to tackle a college course?
The short answer is, read on...

Chapter 2
Believing in yourself

If you are definitely interested in going to college but have reservations about whether you are the right type, whether you have sufficient mental ability, and whether you could cope with the necessary changes in your personal and domestic life, then you need to get these worries into proportion before you start.

Don't feel guilty

Of course, if you are already a working woman you will have faced many of these problems before you start being a student. But if you are a full-time housekeeper and childminder, you may be secretly ashamed of wanting more from life than this. Are you wondering if you can do the right thing by your family if you do the right thing for yourself? Do you think that by becoming a student you will suggest to your partner and children that they are not sufficiently important to fill your life? Or, if you are living with elderly parents, or have relatives who are ill and need a lot of nursing and support, do you expect them to resent your spending less time with them when you develop interests outside your home?

Whatever your domestic arrangements, unless you are carefree and have no dependants you are bound to have considerable doubts about 'abandoning your responsibilities' as the caring person in the household. Most women experience feelings of guilt when they leave their dependants for long periods of the day, and if you become a student you will have the additional problem of having to concentrate on your studies for part of the evenings.

These patterns of conscience are laid down in childhood, and your conscience is bothering you now with ideas based on certain assumptions you took from other people. So it is time for you to revise your opinions of what is right and wrong in the light of your adult experience. You've probably done your best for your family up to now, and intend to do your best in the future, so why should you feel guilty about wanting to make some changes in your life to suit yourself?

To overcome guilt feelings about not being contented with what you have, you need to convince yourself that you have a perfect right to want something different. You need to hold fast to the belief that education is the right of everyone who wants it, either as a means of self-fulfilment or in order to pursue a career. In this way you can avoid being pressured by the disapproval of others who may in fact be concealing their envy of your independent spirit.

Some human rights are basic, but most women seem to find it hard to accept that these rights apply to *them*. Women are so conditioned to the view that they should provide love and security for their families, that they sometimes forget their own needs. Think about the following rights:

The right to decide which needs are most important for yourself
Up to now, you have been the caring, nurturing person in the family, looking after husband, children, parents, or anyone else for that matter. You are helping them to achieve what *they* want in life, so why should they not help you to find an independent identity through education and a career, if that is what *you* want in life? To accomplish things for yourself as well need not involve detaching yourself from your family responsibilities, though you will have to get others to share them. Lots of women have already done this, and you can too.

The right to regard your own needs as equally important to those of others
In making plans to take a college course, you will have to put your own needs on a par with those of your family. The problem will arise constantly, in relation both to large and small decisions, if in the past you made the family's needs your first priority. One way for a woman to handle conflicting demands is for her to take note of the way a man tends to manage when he is left alone to cope with the house. Clutter and mess don't seem to worry most

men as much as they worry women. No doubt we all know some man who is obsessively tidy, but in general it is true that from early childhood girls are taught that dirt is evil, whereas boys are taught that it is all right to make a mess. Girls learn that the kitchen should be spotless and the menu varied: most men feel that if the kitchen is reasonably tidy and there is some food on the table, life will go on. So take a leaf out the men's book, and don't make yourself a martyr to housework.

The right to say 'no' without feeling guilty or selfish
This is yet another way to stop yourself always putting the interests of others before your own. This is very difficult if you have been brought up to think that unstinting service to others is the finest sort of behaviour. But that way you can soon end up with no time to call your own. I am not advocating that you suddenly become completely selfish, or ignore genuine cries for help. But you must make it clear that you are not going to be available at all times without hesitation to attend to the needs of others. If you become a student, those with whom you live have to know that you must not be disturbed for trivial matters when you are studying. They will soon understand that if you say 'no' to a request for help, you have good reason, and you must not feel guilty about the refusal.

The right to be treated as a capable human being and not to be patronized
Do you usually adopt a submissive attitude towards your husband, your parents or your friends, always assuming that they know better than you, and accepting their criticisms without defending yourself? Well, as a student you will have to learn to stand up for your opinions, and if you want to do this without making enemies you need to learn to assert yourself without being aggressive about it. This can only come with practice, but you can help yourself by acting out discussions and debates. For example, imagine that you are being criticized for your decision to become a student and take a government grant to help you financially. Think of some of the nasty things people might say to you about taking a college place which might have gone to a young person, or about living on *their* taxes, and rehearse

your arguments in support of your right to be a mature student. Tell yourself (and the person attacking you) that you have a perfect right to go to college if you are accepted for a place, that you and your family have been paying taxes for most of your life (directly or indirectly), that education should be available for everyone – including your critic – and that you feel you have something to contribute both to college and to society.

The right to state unpopular opinions
You can't conduct an argument if you worry all the time about 'rocking the boat' or believe that 'if you can't say something nice, you shouldn't say anything at all'. Don't feel that, because you are a woman, you must not show that you can argue. A woman who tries to please everyone is probably pleasing no-one, and she will certainly not be respected for her opinions.

If, as a student, you want to take a stand on a matter of principle, or say something that you think might be shouted down, try writing down beforehand what you want to say, and how you will say it. Try out your 'script' on a sympathetic friend.

The right to make mistakes
Experience is the name we give to our mistakes, as the saying goes. So be the kind of person on whom nothing is lost. Read, observe and explore everything in the context of being a student of life. You add dimensions to your experience all the time, and our mistakes can teach us more than our successes.

The right to want to be successful
There's nothing wrong in being a woman and also being ambitious. Don't be afraid of being called 'aggressive' or 'a go-getter'. Just think of yourself as what you are – a more interesting person for having your own interests and aspirations. Other people might try to put you down by calling you names, but you'll have to ask yourself why they are doing this (it could be envy or pure malice). As a student, you will constantly face the problem of how to keep up high work standards without getting upset when your efforts are not apparently rewarded. It is hard to pretend that you don't care what marks you get for an essay, for example, if you have worked really hard on it. But in some cases

you will probably have to be the judge of what you are achieving: if you are doing what pleases and rewards *you*, you don't need to feel annoyed if your teacher doesn't rank your work highly. As long as you learn from your mistakes, it is all part of the process of learning.

The right to ask for help

Don't be too proud to ask for help. It may be a new idea for you to ask your family to help you, and it may seem equally unfamiliar for you to ask help from teachers and tutors. But if you show that you are aware of your limitations, and are willing – despite failings and lack of confidence – to try to do better, you will be surprised how willing they are to help you.

Get your partner to help you, or your parent or a friend, by reading over your essays. In explaining to them what is not clear, you will be forced to state your case more lucidly.

Tell your children when you are feeling down or overwhelmed with work, and ask them to rally round with help and a bit of love. A moment off for a hug won't spoil your concentration.

The right to change direction if you need to

Your college course may not work out exactly as you plan and you might feel guilty about wasting time and money. But instead of spending time on regrets, work out what you want to do as an alternative. Most colleges and universities have academic and/or personal tutors or counsellors to advise you on how to go about it.

The right to express anger

Women have usually been taught that showing anger is not a good feminine way to behave. Yet they are often expected to absorb the anger of their parents, partners or children (whether directed at them personally or at the behaviour of others).

When you become a student and have both domestic and academic work, you must make sure that your family understands that you, too, have a right to blow your top about things that seem unfair, and to get a sympathetic hearing from them. But try to make clear that your anger is directed at the world outside, not at them.

It's never too late ...

Do these rights add up to anything?
If you believe in these rights, and start to live by them, you will:

- feel free to say, "This is me. This is what I feel, think and want";
- feel free to go after what you want by way of education and training, aware that you may make mistakes, and willing to accept your limitations, but at least trying to make things happen *for* you instead of waiting for them to happen *to* you.

Recognize the skills you have

Now you need to convince yourself that you have the ability to cope with the work involved in further or higher education. Instead of dwelling on all the things you can't do, think positively about what you *can* do. Why not start by writing out a list of the skills and talents you have developed so far in life? We all have a variety of abilities which we have acquired at home and at work that we often take completely for granted.

Home

- As a housewife and mother, or simply as someone running a home, you will have dealt with shop assistants, school teachers, town hall officials, doctors, dentists, hospital staff, for example. So you have first-hand knowledge of the problems of dealing with large-scale, bureaucratic organizations and official attitudes. If you become a student of a social science subject you will find that social scientists constantly discuss these aspects of society, and you will be able to identify the difficulties.
- As a result of housekeeping and purchasing goods large and small you will know about:

    budgeting money (or failing to do so) and living with the results – useful if you study accountancy or maths;

    banking practices and how to borrow money, the rates of

Believing in yourself

interest for paying off debts, and the best sources from which to borrow – useful if you want to work in banking or business, or for local government or the civil service;

taking out insurance of various kinds (on the car, on life, etc.), entitlement to national insurance benefits and what is not covered – useful if you want to work for an insurance company or the Department of Social Security;

childcare practices in the home, or in play-groups, or in nursery schools, including your own theories about bringing up children – useful if you study psychology or education;

how to compare various products and consumer goods that you have bought over the years – useful if you study marketing, law or business studies.

- If you are mad keen on hi-fi equipment, you can think seriously about a course in electronics.

These skills that you have developed are not trivial: you have acquired standards by which you can judge the quality of goods and services, including the provisions of the welfare state such as schools and hospitals. You have tested things for yourself, and can speak from practical experience about how far the reality matches the public image or the advertising. You are no doubt used to the idea of consulting a book to find out ideas on changes that are being proposed (perhaps to check on the legal position of a divorced person, or to find out what local system of school reorganization is being proposed, or to find out your benefit rights). This is evidence that you have a mind open to new ideas, and it will be invaluable to you as a student.

If you think that being at home with small children doesn't teach you anything valuable, remember the story of a female vice-president of the world's largest advertising company, who re-entered advertising when her son was 12 years old, having stayed at home since he was born. She said that even the perimeter of a baby's playpen can be a fertile training area, because when she went back to work she found that her experience in handling a small child's temper tantrums worked beautifully when she had to deal with the bad temper of adult colleagues who were under constant pressure. She says she learned with her child to remain calm, stay consistent, and not change her story, and eventually the bad temper evaporated: in dealing with adults she adopted the same tactics.

Work

Another way of documenting your experience is to describe *any* jobs you have done in your life, whether paid or voluntary (and however lowly you consider them to have been). You must have gone through an interview for any paid job. Did the person interviewing you give you a good idea of what the job involved? Were you misled in any way? Would you now know some searching questions to ask a prospective employer? Think about any job training you received, either from fellow-workers or on training courses. What did you think of the methods of teaching? What responsibilities did your job involve? Did you do extra work that was not strictly part of your duties? Women often claim that they are expected in jobs to do things for which they are not paid.

You probably now know the difference between the formal rules of a factory or office or any other workplace (what the bosses say should happen) and the informal rules (what *actually* happens). You know how difficult it is to make people do things they don't want to do, the effort needed to change things, and how important it is to get cooperation from fellow workers. You have probably learned something about trade unions, and have a clear idea of their functions.

Now think what you have learned from doing voluntary work:

- If you have been a fund-raiser, what have you learned about the psychology of fund-raising? Could you prepare the material for a fund-raising campaign?
- If you have done counselling work (say, for marriage guidance, the Samaritans, or the Citizen's Advice Bureau) have you gone through a formal training course? What did you learn from it?
- If you have been active in a political party, have you learned to 'sell' your party's ideals to potential voters? If not, why not?

Believing in yourself

- If you sit on voluntary committees, have you learned to argue for your opinions? Can you hold your own against opposing views?
- If you are, say, a school governor or belong to a management committee, have you been on appointing committees and learned to evaluate people's references, or to understand job specifications?
- If you have been a club or society treasurer, can you keep and present good and accurate accounts?
- If you help at a pre-school playgroup, have you taken a suitable training course? Did they teach you some new ideas about the way children learn?
- If you support any good cause, could you write a persuasive letter appealing for help for that cause?

If you have developed any of these skills, or acquired some of this knowledge, it will be very useful to you as a student, either as a member of student societies or the student union, or in general discussions, or as material for essays. You will have much to contribute in seminars, particularly in subjects such as the social sciences (politics, economics, sociology, social administration, psychology, education) but also as background to literature and modern history, for example. The ability to express your opinions clearly, whether orally or in writing, is one of the most difficult to acquire, so make use of the skill if you have it.

As a student, you will not, of course, be encouraged to relate personal anecdotes as valuable contributions to discussions. That is generally frowned upon, especially in university circles. But starting from your own life, you can gradually weave connections and become involved in theory building, taking a step back from your own experiences to look at the lives of other people. Even if you feel that you have failed at some of the things you have attempted so far (marriage, love affairs, bringing up children, running a business, the jobs you have done), you can try to see where things went wrong and why.

By now, you should have a fairly full idea of the things you *can* do, and although you may originally have thought it a boring chore to list them, at least by now you should feel that you have made a move towards believing in yourself. At all events, you

It's never too late ...

have survived good and bad times, and if you are reading this book it means you are trying to find a new direction in life. So give yourself a pat on the back for initiative.

Don't undervalue yourself, when you are trying to decide whether or not you could be a mature student. Only time will tell whether you can handle an advanced college course, but you can certainly take some introductory courses if you want to. You have a lot going for you by way of skills and knowledge that you have acquired over the years.

Chapter 3
Choosing a course

Where to begin

Welcome aboard! You've decided to become a student, and you are wondering how to choose a suitable course. First you have to decide at what *level* of study you want to start. Don't be scared to try something you know will be difficult, because at the end of the course you want to feel a sense of real achievement. But consider the following questions before enrolling for a course:

- Do you want help with the basic techniques of study? In other words, do you want someone to help you get used to studying again? If so, you should look for a return-to-study course.

- Do you want to learn new skills for a job? If so, you should look for a return-to-work course.

- Do you want to take General Certificate of Secondary Education (GCSE) or A level examinations as a definite route to a degree course? These are advertised as such.

- Do you want to do full-time or part-time study?

There are possibilities for everyone in the field of further and adult education, but some areas of the country are much better served than others. To find out what is on offer in the area where you live, you'll have to *ask around*, and get hold of some up-to-date details, so:

Ask at your local library, or the Citizen's Advice Bureau, for information on what adult courses are running locally.

Ask your local library to show you, or tell you where you can look at, the *CRAC Directory of Further Education* and *Second Chances, a National Guide to Adult Education and Training Opportunities*.

Ask your library for the addresses of local colleges of adult education, colleges of further education, the Workers' Educational Association, and University Extra-Mural Departments or Adult Education Departments.

Ask if there is an Adult Education Information and Guidance Centre in your area. If there is, you can get all the information you need there.

Don't feel that, because you need a lot of guidance in these early stages, you are not really suited to further education. Confidence comes from realizing that there are techniques to be learned which will get you started on the right path. If you need help to familiarize yourself with the common elements of study – taking lecture notes, reading quickly and with understanding, how to write essays – you should look for a course which deals with these skills (and also read Chapter 7 of this book). Older students are usually highly motivated to succeed, and are ready to put a lot of effort in, but they sometimes need to find out what kind of effort is required, and what direction to be aiming for. If you don't get these basic techniques right, you might flounder around for the whole course, and quite mistakenly think you are not capable of getting over the difficulties.

Making contact with a college

Don't be put off if some of the colleges you approach for information about courses for mature students are not too helpful or friendly.

There is research evidence that some women have been frightened away from further education as a result of their first experience in trying to get information about suitable courses. It would be a big improvement if the colleges themselves would train their receptionists and switchboard operators to be more sympathetic and informative to older women who get in touch with them for advice.

So try again if your first approach is off-putting. Take along a friend for moral support when you call at a college for information. If you prefer to telephone, ask for the tutor in charge of

Choosing a course

mature students; if there isn't one, ask who *is* in charge of enrolling mature students; if s/he is not available, get her/his name and write to the tutor personally, asking for an appointment to visit the college and discuss your particular needs. The main point is to get beyond the switchboard operators, receptionists or secretaries, who sometimes see their role as protecting tutors from being bothered.

When you are looking at the details of a particular course in the college prospectus, ask yourself questions such as:

How difficult would it be for me to get on to this course?

Is the college near enough to my home to make travel easy?

Does the course really interest me?

Are classes held at times convenient to me?

Do I think I shall be comfortable at this college?

Can I afford to take the course? (See Chapter 5 of this book)

How can you tell a 'good' college for an older woman?

Does the college show evidence of 'having its heart in the right place' as far as women students are concerned? You could look out for the following hopeful signs:

Special admissions or information and counselling arrangements for mature students and for women.

Special facilities to help older women, such as basic skills courses, childcare arrangements, flexible lecture hours.

Special courses for mature women seeking skills to prepare them for employment.

Courses providing training or re-training for women who are already working.

Women's Studies programmes, or self-help groups where the aim is to develop awareness of the special problems affecting women.

The law requires a college to give women roughly equal

access to courses to that given to men. Course entry requirements must not be based on industrial or employment experience to such an extent that women cannot usually fulfil them. Publicity must not emphasize the 'manliness' of certain courses, and the 'womanliness' of others. Training courses for jobs where women are significantly under-represented can be single-sex. If you think you are being prevented from taking a course solely because you are a woman, you can contact the Equal Opportunities Commission Overseas House, Quay Street, Manchester M3 3HN, for advice about what to do.

So look carefully at the way the college brochure lists courses and entry requirements, and at what special facilities are on offer for women. Ask how many women members of staff there are in the college, and what amenities there are for women students.

Shop around until you find a college which is making an effort to help older women students. You may not have a lot of choice, but sometimes it is worth travelling further to get a more welcoming environment. Some colleges are very keen to get women students, and are looking at the reasons which inhibit women from making full use of their courses. They say the difficulty is not so much how to treat women *as students*, but how to get women through the college doors in the first place.

What options are open to you?

A whole new sector of further education has been developed, with new approaches and new-style courses to meet the needs of older students. It is impossible to catalogue every course on offer, but the major categories are as follows.

Return-to-work courses

Would you like to get a paid job, but haven't a clue what to do? If you want to talk things over with someone, don't be afraid to ask at the Careers Office nearest to you. Their main job is to help school-leavers and college students find jobs, but they will also help *you*. They can tell you about training opportunities, and whether or not you need further qualifications for a job you fancy.

Look for the Careers Office address in the telephone directory, listed under your local education authority.

NOW courses (NOW stands for New Opportunities for Women) are springing up at colleges throughout the country – some are called 'Return to Work', others are called 'Fresh Start' or 'New Horizons', for example. They have one thing in common – to help women who are returning to work after a long gap. The courses tend to be short (usually one day a week for ten weeks) and are geared to boosting your confidence. You don't need any qualifications to go on these courses. Fees vary between colleges and you can often pay in instalments. Your local library could tell you if there is a NOW course in your area.

Employment Training Schemes (ETS) These courses are organized by the Department of Employment, and information is available at your local Jobcentre (look in the phone book for the address). They provide quality training for adults aged 18–59 who have been unemployed for six months, and the chance to gain a qualification or credit towards one. Women who have been out of the workforce for some years, perhaps at home caring for children or others, and now want a job, are also eligible for training. Indeed, there are special arrangements for returners.

There are preparatory courses to help you with reading, writing and arithmetic if you are 'rusty' and cannot pass the pre-entry test. You can learn a completely new skill or can add to skills you already have, to improve job prospects. You could train in non-traditional jobs like car maintenance or lorry driving. Preparatory courses are not meant to be academic but practical and immediately useful, and they can also be a step in the right direction for women wanting to gain confidence in their abilities to tackle *some* formal scheme of education. For many women, setting foot inside any building that smacks of 'school' atmosphere may seem like doing a colossal U-turn. But having taken the first step, some of you will perhaps go on to courses not connected directly with work, when you find that you can cope with – and indeed enjoy – the basic study.

Training in work-related basic skills, or English for Speakers of Other Languages (ESOL) are available. The Training and Enterprise Council (TEC) contracts with employers, specialist training firms, colleges of further education, local authorities and voluntary bodies, to provide these courses. Whether you want to know how to run a business, operate a computer, learn management skills or bricklaying, there will be a package to suit you. There are also courses under the High Technology Training (HTT) Scheme.

You will get a training allowance equal to your weekly benefit entitlement at the time you join a training scheme, plus £10 a week (in 1992). There may be help with travel, lodging, childcare and other costs. If you are offered a job during your training, you can accept it and stay in training as well, but you will then receive a wage from your employer.

The Department of Employment now provides clear and comprehensive information about services, in cheerful looking booklets and through friendly staff in bright, comfortable, open-plan offices. There is no need to feel intimidated about going to the Jobcentre.

Government training in Northern Ireland is a bit different. Send for *Start Again: Make a Fresh Start through Education and Training* from the Equal Opportunities Commission, Lindsay House, Callender St, Belfast 1.

Training for a job at college

For many jobs you'll need to train at either a college of further education, technical college or college of art and design. The subjects taught are too numerous to mention here, but your local library can show you directories which list courses all over the country. You might especially like to note the BTEC courses in which half a million people are enrolled at any one time; some are young people but others are adults updating their skills.

BTEC (Business and Technician Education Council) courses which are available in England, Wales and Northern Ireland, contain less theory and more practice than a degree course, qualifying diploma holders for hands-on jobs such as laboratory technician or building-site supervisor. They are perhaps better suited to people who are uncomfortable with the theoretical nature of A levels. You can do horticulture, computing, fashion, public administration, photography, leisure studies, all kinds of engineering, catering management, physics, textiles and much else.

There are three levels of BTEC qualifications: First, National and Higher National. At each level, Diplomas and Certificates are available. Certificate programmes can be studied part-time; Diploma programmes are taken full-time.

> First Certificates and Diplomas are usually taken by young school-leavers, over a one-year period. There are no formal entry requirements.

> BTEC National Certificates and Diplomas generally need two years of study, and entry requirements are *either* a BTEC First Certificate or Diploma *or* four GCSEs at Grade C (or above) *or* other equivalent qualification.

> BTEC Higher National Certificates and Diplomas involve two years of study. Entry requirements are a BTEC National Certificate or Diploma *or* at least one A level and supporting GCSEs at grade C or above. HND courses are offered at virtually all the universities which were formerly polytechnics, and at many colleges.

A mature student may be admitted to BTEC courses without formal qualifications, if the college thinks she can benefit, and credit can be given for 'competence acquired elsewhere'. You would be well-placed, if you shine in your first or second year of an HND course, to transfer to the degree course (in the same subject) which usually runs alongside it.

BTEC's range of Continuing Education modules and programmes for adults offers a short, flexible way to update your skills. Open Learning makes the programmes available to people who do not wish to attend conventional college courses.

The government has set up a body to reform the system of vocational qualifications. Called the National Council for Vocational Qualifications (NCVQ), it has set national standards for four levels of awards. BTEC is working with NCVQ to make sure that all its qualifications fit into this national framework.

Further details of all courses can be obtained from :

BTEC, Central House, Upper Woburn Place, London WC1H 0HH.

For Scotland there is a similar system to BTEC, but it is not exactly comparable. For information you should write to:

ScotVec, Hanover House, 24 Douglas Street, Glasgow G2 7NG (Tel. 041 248 7900).

Applications for full-time and sandwich HND courses at universities and colleges should be made through:

The Universities and Colleges Admission Service (UCAS), P.O. Box 28, Cheltenham, Glos. GL50 38A.

Applications for HNDs in Art and Design courses go to:

The Art & Design Admissions Registry (ADAR), Penn House, 9 Broad Street, Hereford HR4 9AP.

DFH Paramedical Courses. The Department of Health (DOH) gives grants for courses in auxiliary medical work, but only for dental hygiene, dental therapy, occupational therapy, physiotherapy, orthoptics and radiography. Ask at your local DOH office for details.

Courses leading to membership of professional institutions Many colleges offer courses leading to membership of, for example, the College of Occupational Therapists, Accountancy Institutions, the Society of Chiropodists and the Institute of Chartered Secretaries. The courses vary in length and also in their entry requirements.

A number of colleges offer diplomas (for purely *internal* awards, not for national qualifications) which are recognized by professional bodies for exception from their examinations. But when a college claims that its diploma leads to such exemptions, you should always check before you take it that the relevant professional body accepts it. Some colleges *prepare* for certain professions without being officially recognized by the professional institute or association.

Return-to-study courses

If you feel you need help with the really basic aspects of study, look for one of the courses which last for six months or a year. It might involve attendance for one half-day a week, or one evening a week, or three sessions a week at a university or college of adult or further education. Between classes you would be asked to complete a piece of homework, usually an essay. For example, a basic English course would include advice on effective reading, vocabulary work, using a dictionary, planning and note taking, spelling and punctuation, essential grammar and sentence construction, expression, basic comprehension and composition. If you choose a course especially geared to adults, you will find a teacher who understands your special problems and will give you strong support and encouragement until you can take off on your own. Try to find a college where the tutors on such courses have received special training in the teaching of adults (as is the case in some colleges of adult education). These tutors seem to enjoy teaching older students, saying that the atmosphere is relaxed and there is a lack of discipline problems! Some of them will prepare you to sit General Certificate of Secondary Education examinations, if you wish, while others offer no certificate but encourage you to come to terms with your own abilities.

Flexible study courses

This kind of study involves a combination of correspondence courses (also known as 'distance learning') with support from a college of further education. This enables you – if you can't get to a normal FE course, or don't want to – to take the course anyway. What it amounts to is that you do a correspondence course and have a tutor at a local FE college who marks your work. This means you can see the tutor by arrangement; you can telephone the college for help; and you can attend tutorials at college if you wish. And you can take as long as you like over the course.

The FE college buys correspondence course units, usually from the National Extension College, and sends them to you. You can do a whole range of courses, from study skills to GCSEs and A levels and through to preparatory courses for the Open University or, for example, membership of the Institute of Personnel Management. You can take subjects this way which might not attract enough people locally to form a regular class. But on the other hand you will not get any interaction with other students, so it will be a lonely life. So it would suit you particularly if, say:

you are tied to the house with small children and can't get help with child-minding

you have elderly parents to look after

you have family members who need constant attention

you yourself are handicapped

you want to work at your own pace until you build up some confidence.

The number of colleges offering flexistudy is expanding all the time. For an up-to-date list you should write to:

The National Extension College, 10 Brookland Avenue, Cambridge CB2 2HN.

The National Extension College is a non-profit distributing trust which works extensively with the public sector.

Correspondence courses cover all kinds of subjects that may later exempt you from parts of a degree or professional qualification. You can get details from The Association of British Correspondence Colleges, 6 Francis Grove, London SW19 4DT.

GCSE and A level courses

GCSE (General Certificate of Secondary Education) and A level courses are really for people who are thinking of moving on to higher education or need these qualifications for a particular job. If you enrol on these courses you must feel you can cope immediately with formal, structured learning, have a good idea about writing essays, and be ready to take exams. The courses cover a wide range of academic and practical subjects. As a mature student you can take them either at a local school, further education or tertiary college. You can study full-time, part-time or in the evenings. You will have to pay your own fees, but they should not come to more than about £100 a year (in 1992).

If you are allowed to take A level courses at a local school or sixth-form college, you are not likely to get any special help or support: you will simply be offered the facility to sit-in on, or attend part of, the course offered to sixth-formers.

Many older women who want to take a degree course decide to take GCSE and A level courses as a sort of trial run; they feel that if they can't cope with A levels they are unlikely to cope with a degree course. Now, A level syllabi do not always suit older students: a course advertised as 'suitable for mature students' by a college of further education may simply allow older students to do it – it may not be adapted to their special needs, and it may attract mainly 16–19 year olds. To discover this, you could ask a college if it offers any support services to older students.

It is difficult to advise whether or not you should take GCSE and A level exams, since many mature students get into university without them. But it is clear that these exams are a well-worn path to higher education, instantly recognizable to those who make decisions about whether or not to admit you, so there is less argument about them than about other qualifications. Thousands of women have managed taking A levels, and many have done extremely well in the exams. So there is really no need for you to feel afraid of taking them.

Private courses to prepare you for GCSE and A level exams

Some people take courses at one of the commercial 'crammers' or tutorial colleges, to prepare for GCSE and A level examinations. For three A levels, the fees over a year could be as high as £8,000 (in 1992). You are unlikely to pay less than £3,000. The main advantages are considered to be concentrated courses, smaller classes and more flexible hours.

There are thought to be about 700 independent colleges in Britain. The Conference for Independent Education (CIFE), tel. 0223 820797, which includes tutorial colleges and independent sixth-form colleges, can provide information on the tutorial sector. The Council for the Accreditation of Correspondence Colleges (CACC), 27 Marylebone Road, London NW1 5JS, is an independent body licensed by the government. It inspects tutorial colleges before they can gain membership of CIFE. They look at premises, organization, and the quality of teaching and support services. In a competitive field, these colleges survive on their results. It is very difficult to choose between colleges, but since there are so many of them they are clearly filling a need. You can get additional information about independent colleges from:

Truman & Knightly	or	Gabbitas Thring
76–78 Notting Hill Gate		6 Sackville Street
London W11 3LJ		London W1

Many other people use the privately-owned correspondence colleges. Most of these colleges are private companies, using high-pressure sales techniques. They do not impose entry qualifications, and they advertise widely to attract all kinds of people. You can get some protection as a consumer by looking at the prospectus of a correspondence college to see if it is accredited by CACC, as above.

Taking a correspondence course requires a lot of hard work and self-discipline. These courses are mainly about passing exams, whether GCSEs and A levels or membership of professional institutions. You get notes and assignments which you return to your tutor for marking; self-assessment tests to see how you are progressing; model answers written in a way that should help you to do well in exams (students say these are very helpful). It's a lonely life and you have to be determined to stick the course.

Engineering Courses for Women

It's never too late to be an engineer. Since 1987 the government has sponsored special 'conversion' courses for people without traditional engineering entry qualifications. They are mostly for students with A levels other than maths and physics, but also for older people with a GCSE in maths who are practically minded and want a change of direction. The courses are held in universities and colleges and last a year. On completion a student is guaranteed a place on an engineering or technology diploma or degree course.

Teaching at the University of Hertfordshire takes place between 9.30 a.m. and 3.30 p.m., to encourage mothers to apply. The University of North London runs one of these courses for women only, arguing that women are more likely to thrive in a protected environment!

Alternatives to A levels

If you really hate the thought of taking A level exams, but want to take a degree course later, you can adopt one of several strategies: (a) take some courses such as WEA or Extra-Mural classes, which form a valid educational experience in their own right, but are not necessarily meant to help you gain access to higher education and then try to get accepted on to a degree course; (b) take the Open University foundation course which is accepted by some universities as evidence of your serious commitment to study (see next Chapter); (c) look around and see if a college near you offers courses which are alternatives to A levels, making sure, however, that the course *is* being accepted as an entry qualification for a degree course, and by which universities (see below).

In the north-west of England an Open College system has been developed by 10 colleges of further and adult education in Lancashire and Cumbria, in conjunction with Lancaster University and the University of Central Lancashire. Special features of their courses are:

they require no formal entry qualifications

they do not emphasize written exams (at least, not in the early stages)

the cost is fairly low

they provide entry qualifications for Lancaster University, the University of Central Lancashire and four colleges of higher education in the region they might help you gain entry to other institutions which don't insist on A levels.

Hundreds of adult students have successfully returned to study using these courses. Many of the students say they would not have risked the normal A level courses. The fact that there is no emphasis on exams in the early stages seems to help students, though it is still true that if you want to take a degree you will have to get over exam phobia. Some students find when they get stuck in to the course, that the idea of exams is not so frightening. They particularly enjoy the informality, flexibility and supportive teaching, and the opportunity to study with other adults.

The actual courses do not seem to an outsider to be less agonizing than A levels, but the scheme has succeeded in bringing older students who are afraid of exams back to serious study, and that is a fine achievement. At some stage, however, Open College students who want to go on to higher education have to make the jump to higher level work, and for some this can be a shock. The significant acceleration of pace, the more difficult content, the depth and extent of knowledge you have to acquire, make for a great difference between basic studies and advanced studies.

Diploma of Higher Education courses

These are two-year full-time courses for students who don't want immediately to decide on a special subject or career. Two A levels or equivalent are normally required, but mature students are often accepted without these qualifications. The courses are held in some university colleges and institutes of higher education (in England only). The idea is that you start a general course of study, without any commitment to a particular subject. When you get the diploma, you can continue on to a degree, which would take one or two years of further study (if you find you are coping well), or you could start on a professional training course, for example in teaching or social work. It seems that most students who get the diploma decide to go on to take more qualifications.

Many of the diploma courses are, in fact, linked to degree

courses anyway, sometimes following the same syllabus for the first two years. The only real difference between this kind of diploma and a degree course is that if you want to leave the college after two years, you will have a qualification to take with you (i.e. the diploma).

There seem to be three distinct types of Dip.HE courses. First, there are the independent study courses, which allow students to plan their own scheme around a research programme (the University of East London has the most developed course of this kind). Next, and most popular, is the 'supermarket' kind of course, inviting students to choose two or three main areas of study from a wide range of subjects. Finally, there is the more structured course, such as that at King Alfred's College, Winchester, with its compulsory first year and its declared intention to teach all students to be numerate. As you can see, there is a wide range of courses available, and this seems a very promising way for older students without A levels to re-enter education.

Courses at adult residential colleges

As a means of returning to study, and perhaps as a trial run for doing a degree course, do you fancy going to a residential college which is for adults only? There are eight such colleges around the country, long established and offering an academic training, but not training for a specific job.

The courses are mainly in the humanities and social sciences, and there is a strong interest in industrial relations and trade union studies. Hillcroft College has a course which introduces women to science and mathematical understanding and techniques. The teaching is based on small group tutorials, with lectures and seminars, and a lot of essay writing.

If this kind of concentrated study and preparation attracts you, you can write for further details to one or all of the colleges which offer it. They are:

Coleg Harlech, Harlech, Gwynedd LL46 2PU.

Co-operative College (run by and for the Co-operative Movement), Stanford Hall, Loughborough, Leicestershire LE12 5QR.

It's never too late ...

Fircroft College, Selly Oak, Birmingham B29 6LH.

Hillcroft College (for Women Only), South Bank, Surbiton, Surrey KT6 6DF.

Newbattle Abbey Adult College, Dalkeith, Midlothian.
(As part of the cutbacks in spending on education, this college had its core government funding axed in 1990, and now faces the loss of local authority support, so its future is very uncertain in 1992.)

Northern College, Wentworth Castle, Stainborough, Barnsley, South Yorkshire S75 3ET.

Plater College (Catholic Workers' College), Pullens Lane, Oxford OX3 0DT.

Ruskin College, Oxford OX1 2HE.

- All offer one and two-year courses (and sometimes shorter ones).

- Students are normally between 20 and 40 years of age.

- Most of the colleges offer a qualification that satisfies higher education requirements – in other words, having completed a course at one of these colleges, you would be in a very good position to apply for a place on a degree course.

- All the colleges are recognized and grant-aided (with the exception, now, of Newbattle Abbey) by the government. If you get a place at one of these colleges, you will be given a form on which to apply for a grant. You can't apply for a grant until you have been offered a place. Grants cover fees, residence, maintenance and an allowance for dependants.

- None of the colleges asks for formal entry qualifications. Selection is usually made by interview, but you might have to write an essay, and you would probably be asked to produce references.

Teacher training

It may be that some of you remember the time when it was possible to train as a teacher at a teacher training college, earning a teaching certificate after a two-year course. So it should be pointed out that, except in a few special cases, the only way to become a teacher now is to take a degree. So teacher training will be dealt with in the next chapter, which looks at ways of getting a degree.

Chapter 4
Aiming for a degree

Have you ever thought of taking a degree? Why not have a shot at it? It is a high-level course which will require hard work and determination, but there is joy and exhilaration in doing challenging things, and literally thousands of other older women have already taken degrees. So why not show that you've got what it takes, by taking a degree? Try to make up your mind to take a *full-time* degree, the great advantage being that, if you fulfil certain conditions, you will then *automatically* get your fees, plus a means-tested grant towards maintenance, paid by your local education authority (or the Scottish Education Department in Scotland). See Chapter 5 for full information about finding the money to pay for your education.

A degree is a mark of proficiency, awarded to you for completing successfully a course of study at a high level. In the United Kingdom (other than Scotland), first degrees are, for example, B.A. (bachelor of arts) or B.Sc. (bachelor of science), Pass or Honours degrees which usually take three years of full-time study, or four years for a 'sandwich' course which includes one or more periods of practical experience (for example, in technology, languages, business and management). The degree course structure is different in Scotland. Here the Pass or Ordinary degree course takes three years to complete. The Honours course normally lasts for four, or in a few cases five years (for example, modern languages or enhanced engineering degrees with work experience. Even with a degree, you may still have to train again for some specialized jobs (though some courses like medicine or teaching lead directly to a job), but a degree helps to widen your choice of jobs.

Most students enter the older-established universities with A levels or a BTEC qualification, but you can be considered without these 'normal' entry requirements, on the basis of your work experience and evidence of serious commitment to study.

It's never too late ...

Eighteen-year olds with A levels are already a minority in the new universities which were formally polytechnics; students who have entered by non-traditional routes now outnumber them. Generally speaking, the college would want some evidence of serious commitment to study, or perhaps evidence of work experience relevant to the course.

Where can you study for a degree?

1. At universities

2. At colleges and institutes of higher education and various other colleges

3. At home/by post through (i) the Open University (ii) as an external student of London University.

Profiles and pictures of the 80 (in 1992) admitting universities and university colleges, with details of student numbers, accommodation and cost of hall or self-catering places, library and computer facilities, are given in *University Entrance Official Guide*, published each June by the Association of Commonwealth Universities. Twenty-five colleges of higher education, providing courses validated by universities, are also included, and with similar information as given for universities. The guide forecasts the likely entrance-grade requirements for various courses. Currently, law, medicine, English and pharmacy are the hardest courses to get on to, while there are plenty of places in maths, engineering, computing and chemistry. Business and management studies, in which undergraduate courses were rare a few years ago, is one of the most popular areas, rivalled only by the social sciences. Europe is the new dimension to many degree courses.

You can write for a prospectus to any university or college you fancy, and visit by appointment. But remember that prospectuses are marketing devices, designed to entice you to go there. Nearly a quarter of students, in a survey conducted for the *Guardian* newspaper in 1992, said that their university courses did not live up to the promise of the prospectuses. Those in the former polytechnic sector were most disappointed. On the other hand, one in five of all the students surveyed said their courses were better than outlined in the prospectuses. So it would be a good idea to go and see the college for yourself, and talk to other students, before committing yourself. Later in the chapter we will look at some of the colleges most welcoming to mature women students.

Universities

In March 1992, Parliament enacted the Further and Higher Education Act (England and Wales), and an equivalent Act for Scotland. These two Acts provided an historic turning point for the 34 polytechnics in England and Wales and the five equivalent institutions in Scotland. In effect, they abolished the division between polytechnics and universities, gave polys the right to award their own degrees, enabled them to call themselves universities if they wished to do so, and established single funding councils in England, Wales and Scotland to give financial support to all higher education institutions. Those who work in the former polys are the first to admit that a change of name, a new coat of arms and new degree robes will only make a superficial difference, but they hope to overcome the prejudice of those who automatically assumed in the past that universities were better than polys.

Older universities have always awarded their own degrees, but had external examiners in each subject to ensure that those degrees were of uniformly high standard everywhere. Up to 1993, the Council for National Academic Awards (CNAA) ensures common standards in the former polys. Thereafter, CNAA will be replaced by a Quality Audit Unit, which will cover all the old and new universities.

Not many Britons leave a degree course when they have started, and not many fail to get a degree. In other words, there is a very low drop-out rate. You can be sure that a degree from any British university will have national and international standing and value.

Yet the style and feel of universities vary, as do the methods of teaching, learning and student assessment. And departments within universities can be very different from each other. It can be very hard to choose, but the sort of thing you should look at are the following.

The course structure in traditional universities can be:

1. single subject;
2. single subject plus subsidiary course, or major subject plus minor subject(s);
3. joint degree (two equal subjects, e.g. English & History);
4. general degree consisting of a variety of subjects;
5. several subjects of equal weight in the first year, allowing you to choose one of these as major subject in 2nd and 3rd years (usual in Scotland and in the 'New Universities' founded in the 1960s, such as York and Lancaster);
6. sandwich – a course which combines academic study with practical training or supervised work experience.

The course structure in the new universities (former polytechnics) can be:

1. a modular degree scheme in which course changes are usual (modular means you can choose your own programme of studies from a wide range of subjects);
2. a modular scheme in which course changes are permitted only in the first month;
3. single subject;
4. sandwich – a course which combines academic study with practical training or supervised work experience;
5. a flexible scheme which allows a lot of transfer between degree and diploma courses.

The teaching methods A 1992 survey of students, for the *Guardian* newspaper, showed that only Oxford and Cambridge students gave high scores for overall teaching, although the 'new' universities created in the 1960s joined the most famous seats of learning in winning relatively high marks for access to individual tutors and the overall quality of courses, as well as for accommodation, social life, university location and the standards of the buildings. Some of the former polytechnics, where staffing levels

Aiming for a degree

and spending per student were lower, did less well, suggesting that low funding and their determination none the less to offer wider access had affected student satisfaction. This was described as a policy of 'pile them high, do it cheap'. In many of the new universities, the initial or intermediate year of a degree course is franchised out to the local college of further education.

Students preferred small-group teaching, regarded it as the traditional strength of the British system, and did not want to give it up. Half the students at Oxford and Cambridge were in 1992 normally taught in groups of three or fewer; and more than half in the traditional universities, which included the 'redbricks' such as Manchester and Leeds, were in teaching groups of fewer than 12. By contrast, only four out of ten students in the former polys had such a privilege. However, these new universities stick to their mission of providing higher education for the widest possible clientele – and that includes mature students like you. The more practical the subject you study, the more practical the learning will be, with a greater emphasis on 'doing' rather than 'discussing'.

In the long run, changes will affect both old and new universities, because the system is changing so fast. The government has told all universities and higher education colleges to increase the number of students by a third by 1999, and they rose nationally by more than 10% a year in the period 1989–92. This brought in extra money, but not enough to cover the whole cost, so universities have had to cut corners. The result is overflowing lecture halls, fewer tutors per student, queues for refectories and a crisis over accommodation. The University of East Anglia, for example, once attracted students because of its small, cosy feel, but with a large jump in student numbers some classes are now taught in storage rooms. Many universities have expanded into new premises in recent years, and this can involve considerable travel between sites. In such a case you would need to ask whether free and frequent transport is provided between sites, and what sort of distances are involved.

The assessment methods vary:

1. final examinations only;

2. examinations at the end of Part 1 (taken at end of 1st or 2nd year) and at the end of Part 2 (end of 3rd year);
3. course units (assessed by examination and/or project work), sometimes called modules;
4. continuous assessment (most of the work you do counts towards the final result);
5. a combination of examinations and continuous assessment.

The trend in recent years has been away from traditional exams and towards continuous assessment and assignments. An increasing number of courses are taking into account the previous experience of students, and enabling mature students to be credited for previous work and qualifications. It is worth checking this.

Look for a subject you want to study, in a course which suits you. It is possible to take few examinations, and to specialize or generalize as much as you like.

The so-called 'pecking order'

British degrees are of uniformly high standard, apart from the difference between honours and ordinary or pass degree. So in theory they are equal in value. But there is a well-known 'pecking order': Oxford and Cambridge graduates often get prestigious jobs in universities, the civil service, the media, and big business (the so-called 'glittering prizes') more easily than do graduates of other universities. London graduates come next, followed by graduates of the civic universities and the new universities. Of course, the level and class of degree obtained is also important, as is the reputation of a particular department and its staff and research (and Oxbridge does not have the best reputation in all subjects, nor are all Oxbridge graduates clever or successful!).

British universities are becoming more like the large impersonal European ones, where students are left to sink or swim. Because there is little prospect of any future government paying out significantly more money for higher education, radical alternatives to the current system are being examined. Should British students attend local universities while living at home, thus cutting the cost of maintenance grants? Should universities provide summer courses which enable students to get a degree in a shorter time? Should it be possible to get an Ordinary degree in two years, instead of an Honours degree in three? Should the system of awarding first, second and third class degrees be dropped? Should postgraduate students be used as teaching assistants? Should there be more use of computers and student-centred learning techniques? Universities are in a ferment over these issues.

There is a lot of snobbery and uninformed talk about the prestige of universities, so find a course that appeals to *you*, in a place that is convenient, and enjoy the experience.

Qualifications needed to apply for a university place

It is important to remember that *no qualification of any kind entitles* you to a place on a university degree course: entry is competitive. Traditional universities still have the widest choice of applicants, because many people prefer to go there if they can, and selectors tend to look for the best quality students they can get (usually defined by A level results). Now, A levels and equivalents are not an infallible guide to later performance on a degree course, and the judgement of individual institutions when selecting students is not always the best. But they make their own decisions. Most universities have some special arrangements to encourage mature students (over the age of 21), and some make a point of letting in a percentage of older students each year. If you want to go to a particular university department, it would be sensible to find out its policy on older students, and then try to satisfy the entry requirements. You could ask to see the admissions tutor, or the head of department, before making a formal application, and this could save you frustration and anguish later. The university might ask for:

1. The standard minimum qualifications, such as certain subjects at A level, certain grades at A level, certain GCSE subjects. You might be able to offer a Scottish SCE/CSYS, a BTEC qualification, the IB or EB. But many universities and colleges now offer access courses, lasting for a year, leading directly to degree courses, for people who have no A levels. Unless they are job-related, however, these courses rarely carry grants.

2. No formal qualifications, but evidence of structured study, e.g. having taken WEA or University Extra-Mural courses, ONC/OND, an Open University foundation course.
3. No formal qualifications but evidence of relevant work experience.
4. Your completion of special schemes, such as:
(a) Open College courses (alternatives to A levels). See Chapter 3 for details.
(b) The special entry examination for older students run by the Joint Matriculation Board (JMB) of the Universities of Manchester, Liverpool, Leeds, Sheffield and Birmingham. Described in a booklet entitled *A University Degree: A Second Chance at 21+*, which you can get free by writing to The Secretary, JMB, Manchester M15 6EU. The booklet is written in a formidable style, and may be off-putting, but it has been a bible to many older people wanting to take a degree. "You need to think at least a year ahead" is one of their firm pieces of advice. The scheme is as follows:

- If you apply as an older student for admission *to one of the JMB's five constituent universities* (see list above) and your present qualifications do not satisfy their entrance requirements, (which are "at least two A levels"), the Board will consider whether to allow you to enter for a special test of your fitness to enter the university. The test is restricted to one named degree course in one named university. An examination fee has to be paid, if your application to take the test is approved, and if you are successful in the examination you have to pay an additional registration fee.

- Every approved candidate has to be interviewed, and both test and interview are conducted at the university you want to enter. As you can see, the university wants to look you over very carefully before admitting you. If you are thinking of using the JMB special scheme for mature students, you would do well to contact the admissions tutor, in the department of the university you want to attend, before you start completing the application form.

- Don't let this make you too afraid to apply. The JMB say they are anxious to admit any mature student who could profit from a degree course.

Aiming for a degree

Examples of universities which welcome mature students

The Lucy Cavendish College, Lady Margaret Road, Cambridge CB3 0BU. Lucy Cavendish College is the only college of Cambridge University to cater exclusively for women, accepting married or single women over the age of 25. Teachers in the college have experience of the special needs of mature students, and like other Cambridge undergraduates you would have an academic supervisor and also a personal tutor. The entry qualification is two A levels or their equivalent. You would need to live in college in term time.

Birkbeck College, University of London, Malet Street, London WC1E 7HK. A constituent member of London University, it specializes in meeting the needs of part-time evening students reading for first and higher degrees. Students are not admitted straight from school. *Only* part-time students are admitted to first degree courses, so you would not get an automatic grant from your LEA. Fees have risen sharply, as a result of a reduction in government funding, and in 1992 are £496 a year for undergraduates, £990 for postgraduates. The College Charter says that it is primarily for students "engaged in earning their livelihood during the daytime". So, when you enrol as a part-time student, you have to produce evidence that you are *either* earning your livelihood (working for money) *or* your domestic circumstances are such as to prevent you pursuing full-time study. Formal teaching takes place between 6 p.m. and 9 p.m. Monday to Friday during term time, and most students attend on 2 to 4 evenings a week. Degree courses generally last for four years. You apply for admission to Birkbeck by getting an application form from the College. They will consider you without GCSEs and A levels, but would want evidence of mature age study, some of which might count as credit towards your degree. Almost 5,000 students were accepted on degree courses in 1992, double the numbers in 1982. Three applicants fight for each place, on average.

Goldsmiths' College, University of London, Lewisham Way, London SE14 6NW. Situated in south-east London, Goldsmiths' College is not a typical university institution, being financed directly by the Department for Education (DfE). You could choose between a wide range of degrees, courses and diplomas, and it is possible to take a London University degree.

Entrance requirements are the usual GCSEs and A levels, but the college will consider alternative qualifications for older students. The college would give you advice on the possibilities for *you*.

Imperial College, University of London In 1981 Imperial College decided to take up Lord Scarman's call (in his report on inner city disturbances) for positive discrimination, and to admit students from deprived inner city areas who have not got the A level qualifications normally required. The scheme does not specify which students will be eligible, but it is expected that most will come from disadvantaged ethnic minority groups. There is no reason why women from such areas should not apply.

Imperial College, one of the foremost institutions of science and technology in the world, is hoping to find people from deprived areas who, with special tuition, can cope with the rigours of the courses on offer. It is unlikely that more than a handful of people will be admitted in this way in any year, and they will be required to undergo a foundation course before starting on a degree course. But this could be a chance for *you*.

Manchester, Liverpool, Leeds, Sheffield and Birmingham Universities These universities have a special entry scheme for older students, details of which were given above.

Lancaster University "Generally favourably disposed" to applications from properly qualified mature students (through UCCA), Lancaster would consider for admission a student without A levels only if she had successfully taken a recent course of study at a level considered appropriate. This does not sound effusive, but in fact, the university recruits about 10 % of its students from the over-23s.

The university is also willing to consider exempting from Part I of the degree candidates who have certain qualifications (there are no automatic exemptions, but HNC or HND with a final mark of over 60%, a Certificate in Education or a Dip.HE would be appropriate). If you were admitted straight in to Part II, you could get a degree in two years.

Dundee University Mature students with no formal educational qualifications will now fulfil Dundee University entrance requirements if they successfully complete a unique course run by the university's Extra-Mural department. If you live in Dundee, this could be your chance.

The New Opportunities extra-mural course, established in 1980, involves one day a week of study, for three nine-week terms. The course initially attracted 37 people, *30 of whom were women*. The arts and social science faculty agreed to take performance on this course into account when participants with the necessary highers, who had used the course to update their qualifications, applied to the university.

The faculty board has now agreed to accept satisfactory completion of the course as an alternative form of entry qualification. Three disabled and five unemployed people were among the participants who enrolled at Dundee in 1981.

Glasgow University, in association with the universities of Strathclyde and Paisley, and Glasgow Caledonion University, runs a summer school which acquaints mature students, or those from socially deprived backgrounds, with the university and its ways, which can seem very forbidding. This also helps students to test whether their chosen subject is the one they really want to stick with.

If none of these universities is near to you, check your local one to see what their policy is on mature students. The universities which were formerly polys have up to now been the most willing to take the risk of admitting students without A levels.

How to apply for a university place

1.   Remember that the university year runs from early October to the following September. Applications for entry are dealt with during the twelve months prior to October. The UCAS scheme must be used by most UK and overseas applicants who want to

It's never too late ...

take a full-time or sandwich undergraduate degree course, the Diploma of Higher Education or an HND course offered at universities (and certain colleges affiliated to them) and colleges of higher education. UCAS does not take applications for Cranfield Institute of Technology, the Open University or the independent University College at Buckingham.

So, think at least a year ahead!

2.   For official information about most first-degree courses at universities, write for a free booklet, *How to Apply for Admission to a University*, to:

The Universities and Colleges Admissions Services (UCAS)
P.O. Box 28
Cheltenham, Glos. GL50 1HY

Also ask them so send you an application form.

3.   Having looked through the UCAS booklet, you can write to the Registrar of any university you fancy for more details (UCAS cannot give you any academic advice). Ask them to send you *both* their general prospectus (which will tell you about the whole university) and any separate prospectus for the subject department that interests you. For example, the Engineering department may have a separate prospectus from that of the French department. You can choose not more than eight universities or colleges to put on your UCAS application form; UCAS suggests that you list them in order of preference, but some colleges will consider you wherever you put them on your list.

If, because of your circumstances, you have decided you can only go to the nearest university, remember that you can choose up to eight courses at that institution when applying through UCAS. Don't, however, waste your choices by applying for courses for which you don't qualify.

If you are applying for Oxford or Cambridge university, you should also make a direct application to the university concerned. You may not apply to Oxford *and* Cambridge in the same admissions year.

4.   Fill in your UCAS application form. A university makes its

decision whether or not to admit you (or interview you) on the basis of what you put on this form, and you can't alter the details later. Don't send diplomas or certificates in to UCAS; if a university wants to see them they will ask for them. Indicate on the form that you are a mature student, and say if it would be possible for you to live at home (if accommodation is difficult in the university area, this might count in your favour). And if you are suffering from a disability or illness which could put yourself or others at risk, you must give details (particularly important if you want to do a course involving laboratory work or field work).

Use the form as flexibly as possible. For example, insert only the dates of the last school you attended, and then give your work history. Feel free to give an account of your qualifications and study experience, too, and include a statement of your reasons for now wanting to do a degree. Many universities say that since they have to process a large number of applications in a relatively short period of time, interviews have become the exception rather than the rule. Their next best option is to take very seriously what candidates write about themselves on their application forms. They think these self-presentations give clues to the intangible qualities essential to success on a university course – independence, initiative, commitment to crossing traditional academic boundaries, and a clear rationale for choosing a particular course.

5.　　*Find a referee*. One of the most important parts of the UCAS form is the confidential statement made by an academic referee. If you have been attending a further education college or taking a correspondence course, the college head or your tutor would act as referee. If you have not been following a conventional course leading to A levels, try to choose as a referee some qualified person who can assess your potential; s/he will be asked to comment on your personal qualities and motivation, and say whether you are deemed capable of coping with a degree course. You should give the UCAS form (with a stamped envelope addressed to UCAS) to your referee, who will fill it in and send it off.

If for any reason you cannot get a referee, you have to explain this on the UCAS form, sign it and return the form yourself. In any event, don't forget to attach a cheque or postal order to cover

It's never too late ...

whatever fee UCAS asks for. Receipt of the form will be acknowledged.

6.   The decision about whether to accept you is made by the university, not by UCAS. Most willing and qualified applicants get a place, though not always at the university of their first choice. A lot depends on the course you choose, and its popularity at the time you apply, and how good you are. Each university you list will send you either an offer of a place (this could be unconditional, or it could depend on your obtaining certain A level grades or other satisfactory results), or a rejection slip. If you get more than one offer of a place you will be in the enviable position of being able to choose which one to accept.

7.   If you are unfortunate enough to get rejections from all the universities you list, you can use the Continuing Application Procedure (CAP) which UCAS operates. They will automatically send you information about the scheme, which enables you to name four further choices of courses and university, and will then forward your applications or help you choose a university which still has vacancies. This may not be a very helpful point if you have to stay in a particular part of the country.

8.   If you *can* go away to university, there is an UCAS Clearing Operation in late August and September each year, which tries to match candidates to unfilled places around the country, and a large number of people get places at this stage.

Suppose you are asked for an interview at a university

Let us suppose that you are asked to attend a university department for an interview, with a view to admitting you. You may be taking A levels, or you may be without formal qualifications. What would you expect to be asked, and how would you deal with the interview?

You will certainly be asked what you have been doing since you left school, how you came to decide you wanted to go back to study, and what kind of preparation you made for it by way of classes, reading, and so on. When you answer, the main thing is to be yourself, answer truthfully (not what you think the interviewers want to hear), and don't beat around the bush. If you 'dress up' your experience or learning beyond their worth, you will soon be caught out, but if you say straightforwardly what work, paid or voluntary, you have done, what books you have read, or courses you have taken, you will be respected for what you really are and what you can actually do. The discussion may then flow on to what you think of a particular book, or a topic or question in the subject you want to study. Think before jumping in with an answer, and do the best you can, but if you really don't know, say so. Above all, don't waffle. The interviewers are usually trying to see if you can 'think on your feet' and put together an intelligent argument. Oddly enough, as long as it is sensible and plausible, it doesn't necessarily have to be right! They will undoubtedly end by asking you if *you* have any questions, and it is a good idea to be ready with a couple, such as what books to read before you come, what subsidiary courses you will have to take, how the courses are assessed, or even where to live or what sports and societies are available. The interview will probably last no more than half an hour, and it will seem to be over in a trice.

A possible snag about a university degree course

An important point to remember is that *credit transfer* is not usually available between British universities, because each university is so independent of any other, and many of them seem to find difficulty in acknowledging that another university's courses will fit in with their own. Time off from a university degree course (known as intercalating) can normally be arranged if the conditions are compelling enough – your need to look after a desperately sick husband or child, or your having an illness or nervous breakdown, would be regarded sympathetically. But you would have to return to the same university to finish your degree when your period of intercalation was over.

Things may change in future, because the Department for Education (DfE) has been looking at what other countries do about credit transfer, and is expected to come up with some suggestions for action. But at present it would be very frustrating for you to start a degree course at one university, only to find that you have to give it up when you move to another part of the country, because a different university will not give you credit for the work you have done already.

Erasmus An interesting development is the European Community Action Scheme for the Mobility of University Students (ERASMUS), launched in 1987, whereby students studying any subject at a recognized institution can study elsewhere in the EC and receive full recognition of this period as an integral part of their overall course. The scheme has grown fast. It is run from Brussels, but has offices in most EC countries, and also runs an experiment in student mobility based on credit transfer, known as the European Community Course Credit Transfer System (ECTS).

Colleges and Institutes of Higher Education

There are 57 colleges around the country offering very flexible arrangements for getting a first degree. Twenty-five provide courses validated by universities and the others combine vocational and non-vocational courses in ways well suited to students without specifically academic interests or motivations. These colleges are smaller than universities, and would appeal particularly if you like the idea of a small, friendly place to study. They frequently have a majority of women students, and tend to be set in beautiful, but isolated, campuses, with plenty of residential accommodation. They range in size from Luton's 10,000 to small rural and semi-rural colleges like the North Riding College in Scarborough and Harper Adams in Shropshire with 1,000 students. Many offer the Dip.HE course mentioned in the last chapter and Higher National Certificate and Diploma courses validated by BTEC. They have been unkindly dubbed 'the Cinderella colleges' because many students feel they get academically second best on humanities courses, but they have a reputation for nurturing mature students and in fact some will earn university status quite soon. Others will merge with neighbouring institutions, as south-western colleges did to become the University of Plymouth. And still others will seek some form of association with an old or new university. North Cheshire College, Warrington, for instance, awards degrees of the University of Manchester. The colleges are based on the former teacher training colleges, and most teacher training is done in them apart from university postgraduate teaching certificate courses; they have a sound reputation for teacher training, which we will look at first.

Under the Teacher Training Bursary Scheme you can get a bursary for PGCE and two-year B.Ed courses in specific shortage subjects. This bursary is paid on top of student grants and loans. You can get information from TASC Publicity Unit, Elizabeth House, York Road, London SW1 7PH.

Teacher training

The only way to become a teacher now is to take a degree. You can take a university degree, and then qualify as a teacher by a one-year postgraduate course (the preferred route for secondary teaching), or take a three-year B.Ed (bachelor of education) course (four years for honours). But note that by now teacher training is no longer a fall-back for would-be students whose A levels would not secure them a place on a B.A. or B.Sc course. In fact, the minimum entry requirements for the B.Ed are higher than for general degrees in that applicants must have English language and Mathematics GCSEs of grade C or above included in their five GCSEs and two A levels.

- To find out about colleges in England and Wales which offer teacher training, and how to apply to get on to a course, you should write to:

    The Central Register and Clearing House,
    3 Crawford Place,
    London W1H 2BN.

    Enclose a stamped self-addressed A4 or A5 envelope.

    The Central Register does not cover the universities offering the B.Ed (for which applications have to go through UCAS – see information on this earlier in the chapter).

- If you live in Northern Ireland, you should write for information about colleges offering teacher training to (see over):

The Department of Education,
Rathgael House,
Balloo Road,
Bangor, Co. Down.

- If you live in Scotland and want to go to a Scottish college, you should write for information about admission procedures to:

The Advisory Service on Entry to Teaching,
5 Royal Terrace,
Edinburgh EH7 5AF.

Other courses

The main emphasis is on full-time degree work leading to a career in the 'caring professions', the media or public administration. There is some science and technology. To find out what is on offer, you can get a free leaflet from:

Mr G.R. Mann, M.Ed,
Standing Conference of Principals (SCOP),
Edge Hill College of Higher Education,
Ormskirk,
Lancashire L39 4QP.

Or purchase their *Guide*.

The course structure can be:

1. Single subject (e.g. law);
2. modular programme of combined studies (choose your own programme);
3. multi-disciplinary (combining academic study with project work);
4. a general first year 93 subjects), then firm choice of degree programme;
5. all students start with Dip.HE before moving to degree studies.

The teaching methods Lectures, seminars and tutorials. Emphasis is on small group teaching. Colleges tend to have large libraries in relation to number of students, though stocks not always up to date. There may be laboratories, workshops, studios, theatre, music practice room, TV studio, language laboratory and computer facilities.

The assessment methods vary:

1. orthodox exams with an element of continuous assessment which varies from 11% to 60% according to college;
2. orthodox exams, no continuous assessment but wide use of projects.

Qualifications needed

As stated earlier, the minimum entry qualifications for the B.Ed include the provision that applicants must have English language and Mathematics GCSEs of grade C or above in their five GCSEs and two A levels.

Many colleges have special entry procedures for mature students who do not possess the normal qualifications. You might be asked to 'show evidence of recent successful academic study and commitment to a field of work', for example.

How to apply

Prospectuses and application forms for those not included in the UCAS system are available from the college or institute of your choice. Some recruit directly for courses other than teacher training (a centralized admissions procedure operates for all teacher training and many other higher education courses offered).

The Open University (OU)

The OU system (part-time study from home) is clearly attractive and readily available to you. Briefly, some of its major features are:

- It is the only university set up specially for older students.

It's never too late ...

Every adult living in the European Community (and some other countries) aged 21 and over is eligible to study with the OU.

- Almost all the students are older than the usual 18 and 21 year olds you would meet at a traditional university.
- There are more women, and more working-class students applying for OU places now, compared with the earlier years.
- All first-degree students are studying part-time, so you are all in the same boat. Your fellow-students will generally be experiencing similar problems to yours (since they are all older) so there is plenty of mutual sympathy and understanding.
- There are no minimum entry requirements, so you should not have too much difficulty getting in. You don't need A levels, Scottish Highers, the Abitur, a Baccalaureat, or anything else. Everyone starts with a foundation course designed to develop good study habits and general learning skills.
- You can try out OU study to see if you like it. All new undergraduates get a preparatory pack in the autumn, followed by their first two or three months on the course, at an initial tuition fee. In 1993 the fees are £130 (£317.50 for students living outside the UK). If you decide the OU is not for you, that's all you have to pay.
- A wide range of single courses, certificates, diplomas and postgraduate qualifications are offered for those working in commerce and industry, education, health and social services. A new programme of initial teacher training is being developed.
- You can spread the courses over several years, with breaks between courses if you want them. You must complete a credit course within a given time, once you start it, but you can take as long as you like to get the total number of credits you need in order to earn a degree. (To earn a degree, you need 6 full credits; to earn an honours degree, you need 8 full credits.) You earn a Bachelor of Arts (B.A.) degree whether you take Arts or Science based courses.
- All the courses last nine months, from February to October. A full-credit course involves ten to fifteen hours' work a week, while a half-credit course involves the same amount of work spread over two weeks.

Aiming for a degree

Where are the snags?

- You need a lot of willpower, and you need to like working and studying mainly on your own. You will be committed to studying for up to six years, though you can of course stop whenever you want to.
- You will not automatically get a grant of money to cover course fees etc., because it is part-time study. Some LEAs make grants to needy OU students, and many will pay the cost of OU Summer School because it counts as residential study away from home, but some refuse to finance any OU studies. Elsewhere in Europe the possibility of financial help should be explored locally.
- According to the OU Students' Association, you will pay fees higher than those paid by a part-time undergraduate in a traditional university. Continuing inflation makes it difficult to forecast fee levels for future years, but in 1993 your first year's study, including a residential school and allowing for books, materials, travel, postage, etc., might cost about £475 (or about £855 for students living outside the UK). The OU has a hardship fund, and will for example assist unemployed people. You can pay OU fees by instalments, and 'Fee Loans' are available.
- Some students obviously find OU courses difficult, and there is a high drop-out rate.
- The fact that some OU transmissions on radio and TV take place very early in the morning or late at night causes problems for some students, because few people are at their best *both* early and late in the day. Even the early evening lectures can disrupt family relations or interfere with mealtimes.

Would the OU suit a disabled student?

The OU has about 4000 students who, by reason of a major or even quite minor disability, experience some difficulty in participating fully in every aspect of their courses. The OU takes whatever practical steps it can to assist such students – but this can only be done if you identify your difficulties when you apply.

It's never too late ...

They offer short preparatory courses on study methods for blind and deaf students, advice on how to obtain aids and equipment, special arrangements for exams, special facilities at summer schools (you can be accompanied by your personal helper, for example, or can be excused attendance altogether). Help with transport and with reading is given to blind students by fellow students.

If you are disabled and are thinking of enrolling for the OU you should get in touch with the Director of Social Services of your local authority, to see what financial support to cover special needs might be available under the Chronically Sick and Disabled Persons Act, 1970.

Are OU degrees as valuable as those from other institutions?

- They are validated by the same external examiner system (many examiners being on the staffs of traditional universities). Many universities accept OU credits as the basis of allowing students on to degree courses, and accept OU degrees as the basis for postgraduate studies.
- In a massive survey of graduates, OU students themselves reported that they had benefited significantly form their studies, either by improved skills or better pay or both.
- Employers are usually impressed by the character and perseverance shown by OU graduates, and welcome the flexibility of graduates who have not specialized too narrowly.

If you are considering taking an OU degree, think about:

The course structure You take a general degree, with or without honours. Six full-time credits (or the equivalent in a combination of full and half credits) are needed for the B.A. degree, and eight for Honours. Taking two full credit courses a year (the maximum allowed) you can gain a B.A. in three years and honours in four. However, most students progress at the rate of one full credit or two half credits a year, to complete their B.A. degree in six years. Others take longer.

There are 6 main study areas or faculties: Arts, Educational

Aiming for a degree

Studies, Mathematics, Science, Social Sciences, and Technology. Your undergraduate studies normally begin with one or two foundation courses. After this, each faculty offers a range of courses at second, third and sometimes fourth level. Most second level courses are designed for breadth; third and fourth level are honours standard. You can choose from more than 120 courses, and can combine courses from almost any of the faculties. You cannot concentrate on a single subject, but you can choose closely related ones.

The teaching methods You do most of your work through 'distance learning' (another name for a correspondence course, but with certain additions). The four main parts of an OU course are:

1. *Correspondence materials* – specially written booklets, some notes, perhaps some experiments, exercises and self-assessment tests (so that you can make sure you have understood things) and assignments to write and send back. You will need to buy the set books.
2. *Broadcasts* – radio and TV programmes which relate to the course (each one is broadcast twice). Tapes and videotapes can be seen and heard at local study centres, if you miss the broadcasts.
3. *Tutors, counsellors and study centres* – there are about 250 study centres around the country, usually in further, adult or higher education colleges, and some in the Republic of Ireland and in mainland Europe. Course tutors will hold regular meetings with you and other students; discussions and lectures give you a chance to meet each other too. You will have a counsellor to help you if you get behind with your work or find things difficult.
4. *Summer Schools* – one-week residential courses held on the premises of a university, to give you a taste of the traditional university atmosphere (though you won't mix in with 18 to 21 year olds, who are away on vacation). There are no nursery facilities at OU Summer Schools, so you will have to get someone else to look after the children for the week. If for some good reason you cannot attend the residential school, you will be excused. Documentary evidence is required, however.

The assessment method A degree from the OU does not depend entirely on passing one final set of exams. For each course you take, account is taken of your essays and assignments, and this 'continuous assessment' counts for 50% of the marks; you also take a 3-hour final exam (held at a local centre in October or early November) which counts for the other 50% of the marks. If you don't pass the exam, however, you are very unlikely to get a credit.

You are supposed to get your written work back, marked, from your tutor fairly quickly so that you know how you are doing. OU students say this counsel of perfection is not always followed, but remember that OU tutors are usually doing the work in addition to their major job. You should expect to get the work back within a month. Assignments consisting of multiple-choice questions are often marked by the central computer. The best of your grades are used at the end of the course, in assessing your performance.

How to apply for the Open University

For detailed information about courses, and for the application form, write for the *Guide to the B.A. Degree Programme* to:

The Admission Office, Open University,
P.O. Box 48, Milton Keynes MK7 6AB.

The earlier you apply for an OU place, the better your chance of getting one. For example, the closing date for study commencing in 1993 was 30 September 1992, but months before that they had received sufficient applications to fill all the places available. Apply first, and seek answers to your queries later! You can withdraw the application if you change your mind.

Your application form is passed on to the regional office of the OU, who may telephone or write to you; or you might be invited to discuss your application at your local study centre (but this is not a selection interview).

When the OU has processed your application, they send an acknowledgement letter with your personal reference number, telling you if any of your course preferences are no longer available, but otherwise confirming your choices. Places are allocated in a series of phases between March and the end of July, and they try to keep a balance between regions and the sexes. Precedence is given to people who applied in previous years, but were turned down. Forty-five % of applicants get places.

Between March and the end of September you hear the outcome of your application. To accept an offer you sign and return the agreement, pay the appropriate fee, and initially register for the course. Final registration takes place the following spring.

Links with other institutions

1. Credit for study completed elsewhere

- *Credit exemptions* You *may* be awarded some credits towards your OU degree on the strength of having successfully completed one or more years of full-time study (or part-time equivalent) at an educational level higher than A level, Scottish Higher, ONC, Abitur or Baccalaureat. The maximum is three exemptions.
- *Direct credit transfer* If you have successfully completed:
  (i) part of a CNAA degree;
  (ii) whole or part of a Dip.HE course at a College of Higher Education or elsewhere;
  (iii) one or two years' study at one of the many universities, including Essex, Heriot-Watt, Lancaster, Hull, Kent, St Andrews, Salford, Stirling, Southampton, Strathclyde, Sussex or Wales, which have agreements on this with the OU.
  The OU may count these periods of study towards a degree with them, up to a maximum of four credits. You can get full details of these advanced standing arrangements from the OU.

2. Links with traditional universities

These are now being made. For example, Lancaster University and the North-West Region of the OU have launched a joint facility exchange scheme which they hope will benefit mature students like you. Each university has agreed to make certain facilities available for use by mature students from the other. Lancaster, which has all the facilities of a full-time campus university catering for over 5,000 students, is now offering OU students a range of services, including use of the library, access to advisory services such as counselling and careers, and attendance at university lectures. OU students can also join in campus activities such as concerts, the indoor recreation centre and the theatre studio.

3. OU students entering universities
Many traditional universities accept the OU foundation courses as valuable evidence of serious commitment to study, when offered by students who have no formal entry qualifications.

London University External Degree Scheme

This is the oldest way of getting a degree part-time, and it is open to students from all over the country. It takes a lot of hard work and determination, but thousands have done it.

The course structure offers traditional single subject degrees, or joint degrees. You cannot make any major change of direction during the course, so you need to be quite sure about what you want to do. Registration is valid for a maximum of eight years; five years should be considered a reasonable minimum period for getting a degree.

The methods of teaching No teaching is offered. It is up to you to take a private correspondence course, or evening classes at a private or LEA college. You make your own enquiries and decisions about how to prepare yourself for examinations. You need to be near good libraries, and to spend a lot on books.

The methods of assessment There is one final examination for single subject degrees. For joint degrees there is an exam at the end of each separate subject. Exams do not differ in standard from those of internal students.

Consult *Regulations for External Students*, published each year by London University in September/October, and available at public reference libraries. Make sure you look at an up-to-date copy. Or write to:

Aiming for a degree

The Secretary for External Subjects,
University of London,
Senate House, Malet Street, London WC1E 7HU.

Qualifications for entry

These are normally stated in terms of GCSEs and A levels, and are detailed in a pamphlet *Regulations for University Entrance*. You can get a ruling on your individual position by writing to The Secretary for Entrance Requirements (address as above) giving full details of your present qualifications and saying which course you hope to study. There is a charge of £10 for checking whether entrance requirements are satisfied; if they are, a Statement of Eligibility is issued.

How do OU and London External degree courses compare?

- London University prefers you to have A levels; the OU has no entry qualifications.
- External degree fees are cheaper than OU fees.
- The OU gives you a correspondence course and a tutor, and a local study centre where you can meet other students, as well as a Summer School. External students taking London degrees don't get any teaching (except through the Commerce Degree Bureau which provides correspondence courses in preparation for the B.Sc. (Economics) Examination).

Checklist

1. You can apply to any college you fancy, to take a degree course, whether or not you have GCSEs and A levels. If you don't have them, you stand a better chance of being accepted if you are following some course of study at a reasonably high level, thereby proving that you are a serious student. Obtaining a degree is like travelling to the city centre. If the most direct route is blocked, there are back ways to reach your destination.

It's never too late ...

2. Some universities and colleges make themselves more open to older students by having special entrance schemes. For example:

professional and technical qualifications may be accepted as equivalent to GCSE exams;

the college may set its own tests;

the college may let you in on the strength of an interview alone.

Read the prospectuses carefully.

3. The Open University was set up specially for older students. It has no entry requirements, and runs courses to get you used to studying before you start the degree course. Between 1970 and 1990 the number of students in part-time higher education in the UK more than doubled. In 1990 women accounted for 42% of these students, compared with 14% in 1970.

4. If you are willing to organize your own preparation, and have the necessary GCSEs and A levels, you can take a London University External Degree.

5. You can look for certain signs in the prospectus of any college, indicating that older students are made welcome, such as:

- Do they *say* they welcome older students?
- Do they provide accommodation for married students?
- Do they have childcare facilities?
- Do they have hours and teaching methods which take family responsibilities into account?
- Do they run part-time or evening courses?
- Do they provide refresher courses designed to help students who have left school for some time?
- Do they have a sympathetic approach to women's lack of confidence about taking courses which mainly attract men students?

Chapter 5
Finding the money

What do you need money for?

It costs money to study, whether you pay for it yourself or get someone else to pay for you. You need money for:

>*tuition fees*
>*examination fees*
>*travel to and from college*
>*college fees (at collegiate universities only)*
>*student union fees*
>*meals at college*
>*books*
>*equipment (pens, writing pads, file covers, a calculator, maths instruments, perhaps protective clothing)*
>
>*and*, if you are taking a full-time course, you may need money to support yourself (and perhaps your family), depending on your personal circumstances.

Overseas students may be expected to pay the full cost of their education. However, European Community nationals will be eligible to pay the same lower fees as home students, and to have them reimbursed by the UK government, subject to certain conditions.

Who gets money for study?

Money is available from various sources, mainly from the government but also from private funds. Older women students are treated exactly the same as other students. The main point to bear in mind is that *it is the course which attracts the grant*, not you as an individual (though the amount of grant, if awarded, will depend on your means). You will not get mandatory grants or loans for

It's never too late ...

- postgraduate courses – except postgraduate initial teacher training;
- courses that are part of the 'Articled Teachers Scheme';
- nursing courses under the 'Project 2000' schemes;
- courses of further education, such as A levels, Scottish Highers, City & Guilds awards, BTEC and ScotVec National Awards (these are different from Higher National Diplomas); and
- part-time courses – except some initial teacher training courses.

The large groups of students getting grants are on:

(a) Employment Training Schemes offered by the government, for which weekly allowances are paid (see below);
(b) courses designated by Local Education Authorities (LEAs) which carry mandatory or discretionary grants (see below for definitions).

When you are in doubt about whether your LEA will give a grant, don't hesitate to apply for one and see what they say. It is up to you to start the ball rolling. Make enquiries about a grant even before you have the offer of a firm place on a course. LEA award regulations are complex, and the criteria for awarding grants to mature students are not always clear. So, if taking a course is only possible for you if you get a grant, make sure that the course entitles you to a grant.

Your college will not usually take any part in applying for a grant on your behalf. However, some colleges have their own scholarships and bursaries, which they award out of private funds. And some colleges are prepared to waive fees in certain circumstances. So you can always ask the college if it can do anything to help you.

Where do you apply for a grant?

Local government

England and Wales. You apply to your local education authority (LEA) for information about grants. You can find the address in the telephone directory under the name of the County (or similar) Council Education Committee. LEA grants cover most full-time degree courses, and some courses in further and higher education. You apply to the LEA *in which your home is located*, which may or may not be the one where your college is located.

You can get a copy of a brief guide to grants and loans from the DfE, Publications Centre, P.O. Box 2193, London E15 2EU. The Welsh Office Education Department publishes a Welsh language booklet on student grants and loans, which can be obtained from the Department for Education at Government Buildings, Ty Glas Road, Llanishen, Cardiff CF4 4WE.

Scotland. Your local education authority, whose address you will find in the telephone directory under 'Regional Council', awards grants to cover courses of a 'non-advanced further education level'.

Grants to cover courses of an 'advanced further education level' at universities, central institutions and colleges of education, are awarded by the Scottish Education Department, Awards Branch, Gyleview House, 3 Redheughs Rigg, South Gyle, Edinburgh EH12 9HH. They issue their own guide, called *Student Grants in Scotland – A Guide to Undergraduate Allowances.*

Northern Ireland. You should write to your local education and library board, whose address will be in the telephone directory, for grant information. A brief guide, called *Awards and Loans to Students,* is obtainable from the Department for Education, Scholarship Branch, Rathgael House, Balloo Road, Bangor, Co. Down BT19 2PR.

ERASMUS (the European Community Action Scheme for the Mobility of University Students) makes top-up 'mobility' grants available to students in inter-university cooperation programmes (ICPs), to help cover the extra costs incurred during study in another country, including return travel, language preparation and cost-of-living differences. These grants are not usually awarded to first-year students.

It's never too late ...

National government

The Department of Employment pays the allowances for job training and retraining courses known as the Employment Training Scheme. Your local Jobcentre is the first place to ask about courses and allowances.

The Department for Education (DfE) pays bursaries if you go to one of the adult residential colleges listed in Chapter 3. When you are offered a place, the college send you a grant application form which you fill up and return to them, and they do the rest.

The Department of Health (DoH) provides grants for courses in auxiliary medical work, for dental hygienists, occupational therapists, physiotherapists, orthoptists and radiographers. Contact your local office of the DoH for details.

The DfE and the Research Councils also provide money to do higher degrees, but it is a very competitive field and grants are hard to get. You need a good first degree and good academic references. Your referees will point you towards the appropriate source of funding.

Other sources of funding

Sponsorship by employers. Over a hundred employers (including the armed forces) offer money to students on Business and Technician Education Council courses (BTEC, ScotVec), higher courses and first degree courses in a number of subjects. To get one you have to agree to work for the employer afterwards for a set time. For a full list send for *Sponsorship offered to students by employers and professional bodies for first degrees, BTEC higher awards, or comparable courses*, published by the Careers and Occupational Information Centre, Dept CW, ISCO 5, The Paddock, Frizinghall, Bradford BD9 4HD. Price £3.56, including postage, in 1992.

Educational charities. Some charities give grants to students. They are usually small, but would help with fees, books and equipment. The Educational Grants Advisory Service can help you look for a suitable charity, and you can write to them: EGAS, National Council of Social Service, 26 Bedford Square, London WC1B 3HU. There are also two directories you can look at in your public library, to find addresses of charities:

Directory of Grant-Making Trusts (Charities Aid Foundation)
The Grants Register (Macmillan).

For which courses are grants available?

To repeat, whether or not you get a grant depends on the course you take. Getting a grant normally means that your fees are paid as well. So which courses attract grants?

Employment Training Schemes – the enormous programme of training and retraining offered by the government.

Full-time degree courses at universities and colleges of higher education normally carry a mandatory grant (see below).

Other advanced courses are 'designated' for mandatory grants (see below).

Some 'non-designated' courses carry discretionary grants (see below).

Courses at colleges of adult education and colleges of further education can only attract discretionary grants, and you are not very likely to get one. But you can apply to the LEA and see what they say. Broadly speaking:
– you almost never get a grant for a part-time course (GCSE, A, or any other level);
– you rarely get a grant for a full-time GCSE course;
– you might get a grant for a full-time A level course;
– you might get a grant for ONC or BTEC First Certificate/Diploma courses (though your employer might sponsor you for these, too). Sometimes a college will waive the fees, for unemployed people, those on supplementary benefit, or those on low incomes. So ask your college if it can help you.

Part-time degree courses do not automatically entitle you to a grant.

Birkbeck College (London University), Malet Street, London WC1E 7HX, specializes in meeting the needs of part-time students and will give you advice on possible sources of financial help. Write for their free leaflet, *Awards for First Degree Courses*. For their own students, Birkbeck has a scheme of awards, operated by a Scholarship Committee.

Part-time teacher training courses sometimes carry a mandatory grant.

Evening classes (or day classes) organized by the Workers' Educational Association, or a University Extra-Mural Department, do not attract grants, though your fees might be waived if you are unemployed or a pensioner.

Courses at independent colleges of further education do not attract LEA grants.

Sandwich courses. Students who do periods of full-time study and periods of associated professional experience can get a grant for the study periods. 'Assisted' students (say, anyone given paid leave from employment to attend a course) receive no grant if their allowance exceeds the amount of fees and maintenance grant.

Courses attracting funding from industrial firms. It is possible for an employer to pay a sponsored student (up to £3,550 in 1992) without this affecting entitlement to an LEA grant.

Grants from LEAs

There are two kinds of grant made by local education authorities (LEAs) in England, Wales and Northern Ireland:
mandatory – the LEA *has* to give it to you if you satisfy the conditions;
discretionary – the LEA does not have to give it to you, but can do so if it wishes.

The LEA is responsible for deciding whether or not you are eligible for a grant, how much grant you will get, and for paying the grant. The Department for Education (DfE) decides the level of grants and provides the regulations governing them.

Mandatory grants

Mandatory grants must be paid to anyone who gets a place on a 'designated course' and meets the necessary conditions (see below). Designated courses are all at advanced level, and nearly all are full-time:

university courses leading to a first degree;

diploma of higher education courses;

HND (Higher National Diploma), BTEC (Business and Technician Education Council) diploma courses (known in Scotland as ScotVec diploma courses), teacher training courses, including the one-year postgraduate certificate in education or the Art Teachers' Certificate or Diploma;

other designated courses (an assortment which might include what you *want to do), comparable to first degree courses.*

For a full list of these designated courses, you can write for the *Guide to Grants: Designated Courses,* from the DfE, Room 2/11, Elizabeth House, York Road, London SE1 7PH.

The main conditions for receiving a mandatory grant are:

- You must ordinarily have been resident in the UK for three years up to the beginning of the academic year in which your course begins (or would have been so resident if you, your spouse or either of your parents had not been temporarily employed outside the UK). Special conditions apply to refugees, and children of migrant workers from the European Economic Community.

- If you are from another EC state, but do not have 'migrant worker' status, you may get an award for just your fees. You must have been living in the EC for the three years immediately before your course begins. You will not be able to get a student loan under the government scheme.

- You must apply for a grant to your home LEA before the end of your first term at college. Most people would apply much

earlier than this, well before the course starts, and you could be refused a grant if your written application does not reach the LEA in time.
- You must not previously have attended an advanced further education course (degree level or equivalent) of more than two years' duration. (A period of up to one term's attendance at such a course is disregarded). This means that if you have completed one course of advanced education, even if you did not then receive a grant, you will not later be allowed a grant to take a different course.

  Note: This condition is relaxed for students who wish to take a course for the Postgraduate Certificate in Education or for the Art Teachers' Certificate or Diploma.
- You must give the LEA a written undertaking to repay any money which for any reason is paid in excess of your entitlement.
- You must not, in the opinion of the LEA, have shown by your conduct that you are unfitted for a grant. No-one seems sure what you have to have done to disqualify yourself in this way.
- You might have to have two A levels (or equivalent) – though older applicants may be excused this condition.

The following will not affect your entitlement to a mandatory grant:
- A foundation course credit from the Open University.
- Certificate of completion of a full-time art, drama, or music course of two years or more.
- OND, BTEC certificate or diploma.
- European or International Baccalaureate.

How much money might you get as a mandatory grant?
Remember that your course fees will be paid automatically.

Figures soon get out of date, but in 1992/3 the maximum grant for full maintenance was:

£2,845 for London students living away from home;
£2,265 for students living away from home outside London;
£1,795 for students living at home with parents.

The grant is means-tested (on your own, your parents', or

Finding the money

your husband's income, according to your age and circumstances), so it can be much less than these maximum figures. Your parents or spouse will be expected to make up your grant if they have enough joint residual income (what is left over after deducting allowances). In 1992, if this was below £13,630 parents would not be expected to contribute anything; if it was £30,000 they would be expected to contribute £2,129. A husband with a residual income below £10,785 would not have been expected to contribute to your maintenance grant, but if he had £25,000 in residual income he would have been expected to contribute £2,082. But there is no redress if the relevant person does not do so, or refuses to give income details to the LEA. Your LEA will ask you to estimate your total income for the coming academic year (all the money you earn or receive, after tax). The following income will *not* reduce your grant:

- the first £3,550 from any scholarship, sponsorship or similar award;
- the first £3,550 from your permanent employers, if they release you, for example on part or full pay, to attend the course;
- any income from casual or part-time jobs during your course; this includes work during the holidays, in the evenings or at weekends;
- the first £1,665 in trust income, depending on your circumstances;
- the first £2,780 of any pension. This does not include disability pensions;
- any social security payment or similar payment;
- any educational payments such as student loans, payments from your college's Access Funds;
- payments under the COMETT, ERASMUS or LINGUA programmes;
- the first £730 from any other sources.

The LEA will reduce your grant pound for pound if you think you will get more than any of those amounts. You become an 'assisted student' if the total payments you expect to get in the year from scholarships and from your employers are the same as or more than your college fees and your total grant entitlement.

It's never too late ...

In this case you will not get an award for either grant or fees. This will not affect your eligibility for a loan. However, you will at least get your fees paid.

In addition to the above grant, the following can be paid:

- excess travelling expenses for some medical, dentistry and nursing students, and for disabled students;
- a contribution towards special equipment for courses;
- extra money for *compulsory* study abroad (i.e. part of your course);
- if you are disabled, you can get higher travelling allowances and possibly means-tested allowances of up to £4,430 a year for a non-medical personal helper; up to £3,435 for the whole of your course for major items of special equipment; and up to £1,110 a year for other extra costs such as tapes and braille paper;
- if you are aged 26 or over and have earned or received (in benefits) a certain specified sum during the three years before the start of the course, there is an Older Student's Allowance. In 1992 this was £280 for a student aged 26 when the course started, £500 for one aged 27, £750 for one aged 28, and £980 for one aged 29 or over.

Your parents will not be asked to contribute to your grant if you have independent status, which applies if you meet *one* of the following conditions:

(a) you are 25 or over before the start of the academic year for which you are applying for a grant;
(b) you have been married for at least two years before the start of the academic year for which you are applying for a grant;
(c) you have been self-supporting for at least three years before you start your course. This includes any time when you were unemployed or on a government training scheme;
(d) both your parents have died;
(e) your parents cannot be traced or it is not practicable to contact them;
(f) your parents live abroad and an assessment would put them in danger (e.g. if you are a refugee);
(g) you are a single parent.

If you have independent status, you may claim a grant for dependants (usually, but not always, a husband and children). The maximum you could get in 1992 was £1,690 for one adult dependant, £1,690 for the first dependent child if you had no dependent husband or other adult dependant; payment for other dependent children ranging from £355 for a child under 11 to £1,350 for a child aged 18 or over. Also, if you have to maintain a home for yourself and a dependant, other than the home you live in when you attend the course, you can get an extra grant of £595 a year.

Discretionary grants

If you do not qualify for a mandatory grant, or are not intending to take a designated course, you may still qualify for a discretionary grant. These can be given for non-advanced courses such as electronic technician, nursery nursing, OND, speech therapy, catering, beauty therapy. You have no automatic right to a grant if you take one of these courses, and it is worth remembering that you can only ever get *one* discretionary grant, so make good use of it if you get one. Incidentally, you would be expected to study locally if a course similar to the one you want to take is available there.

There is no national fixed scale for discretionary grants, and amounts vary from one LEA to another. So you will have to write to your own LEA for details of their particular scheme, and then fill in their application form. You might be asked to attend for an interview at the Education Offices. If you *do* get a discretionary grant, it is particularly important to find out whether or not it covers fees, as these are rising all the time. Most awards (however small) do include payment of approved fees for students who are residents of the UK and the European Community.

Because of the government's financial cutbacks, many LEAs are cutting back on discretionary grants. If your payment is refused, you can ask for the LEA's reasons *in writing*, and you can appeal against their decision to the Education Committee. You should enlist the support of your local councillor if you think you have a good case for a grant.

Note: In Scotland all awards are discretionary, whether for advanced or non-advanced courses. Students on non-advanced courses can be awarded regional bursaries at the discretion of the region. If an award is made, it is in accordance with the Further Education Bursaries Regulations.

Students on advanced courses in Scotland receive awards from the Scottish Education Department (SED). The range of courses for which the SED will make awards is somewhat broader than that which attracts mandatory grants in the rest of the UK, for example certain pharmaceutical courses will attract an SED award. However, if a Scottish resident wishes to study in England or Wales, the SED applies the criteria of whether the course is designated for mandatory awards by the DfE.

Advice on discretionary grants
The National Union of Students, 461 Holloway Road, London N7 6LJ, publishes a *Grants Survey* which would tell you which LEAs give discretionary grants, and for what courses. They know more than anyone else about the vagaries of different authorities.

All the regulations on which this chapter is based are subject to change from year to year, *so you must check up with the LEA* in your home town before making any definite decisions.

How are LEA grants paid?

- If awarded, cheques for maintenance grants are sent by the LEAs to universities and colleges.
- You collect your grant from your college at the beginning of each term *after* you have registered for the course.
- The college sends applications for tuition fees (including college and student union fees) either to your grant awarding authority (or to you if you don't get a grant), during your first term.

Student loans
In 1990 a system of student loans was introduced by the government, to supplement existing forms of financial support. You can apply for a loan once you are attending a course of higher education. All courses that attract mandatory grants also attract

loans. Some courses are not eligible for mandatory grants, but you can get loans for them; they include some courses for the further training of teachers or youth and community workers and some sub-degree courses such as the Certificate of Qualification in Social Work. If you are thinking of taking a course and are not sure whether it is eligible for a grant or a loan, contact the university/college you are hoping to attend for information and the necessary forms.

To qualify for a loan you must be aged less than 50 when your course starts. You must also have a bank or building society that can handle direct credits and debits. You must also promise to tell the Student Loans Company if you stop attending your course before finishing it. You cannot take out a loan for more than one year at a time or for more than one course at a time. But you will usually be able to take out a loan if you attend another eligible course in the future.

The maximum amount of loan that you can get depends on where you live and study. You do not have to take out a loan, and you can borrow any amount up to your maximum, which for 1992/3 was £830 for a London student living away from the parental home, £715 elsewhere, and £570 for a student living with parents. The maximum loan is lower for your final year of study, because it does not cover the summer holidays that year. Loans are not means-tested.

Details about how to apply for a loan, how it will be paid to you, and how you will pay it back when your course ends, are in the DfE pamphlet, *Student Grants and Loans*. For the loans, interest is set once a year at the prevailing rate of inflation in June. Repayments do not have to be made until the April after graduation, or the student leaves the course. And then they can be deferred if your salary is less than 85% of the national average earnings. The student loan scheme is controversial, but bank loans would be a much more expensive way to borrow money. It is interesting that the highest take-up of loans in the first year of the scheme was by mature students.

In real terms, the value of the standard maintenance grant has fallen over time, and it is frozen at the 1992/3 levels. In a survey conducted by the *Guardian* in 1992, three in ten students were finding employment during term time to supplement their grants and loans. University College, Cardiff, has an employment agency providing casual labour jobs around the university to hard-up students. It is very successful but there is not enough work to go around. Students are restricted to 15 hours' work a week. Students at other colleges do night work in local firms to earn money.

The government says it will review the financial situation of students each year, but increases will be provided as loans, not grants. If you study at a publicly funded college and have serious financial difficulties, you can apply for help from the Access Funds which colleges handle. And if you are likely to suffer hardship during a vacation, you may be able to get a Vacation Hardship Allowance from your LEA (this is not available in Scotland).

Other financial concessions and entitlements

Banking facilities. If you have not previously had a bank account, a good time to start would be when you become a student. All the banks compete keenly for students' accounts; most offer free banking to full-time students – while you are in credit or agreed debit – and a cheque guarantee card. Shop around for the bank that will give you the best deal as a student (they vary a lot).

NUS schemes. (a) The National Student Discount Scheme is a standardized discount scheme which includes a discounted membership of the Royal Automobile Club and a good range of discounts on books. Too use the scheme you need to buy a membership card from the Students' Union at your college, and get the booklet listing the shops you can use. (b) Endsleigh Insurance provides reliable, low-cost insurance for students (and others), and covers motor, travel, property and life insurance. You can pay for six months at a time, or get the normal twelve month policy for your car. (c) Your student union can help you find the lowest air travel tickets available. (d) Many local students' unions organize bus travel at weekends, at low prices. You could, as a mature student, take your family along at the same rates (provided that other students do not require the seats).

International Student Card, which you can buy from your student union, is very useful when you go abroad, since you can get reduced admission to galleries, museums, etc.

Reduced prices. There are often reduced prices for students of all ages at local theatres, cinemas and concert halls, and all they ask you to do is produce your student union card as proof. Some of the London theatres also have concessionary rates for students.

Free and concessionary membership of organizations. (a) A student of a college of education or university department of education can get free membership of the National Union of Teachers (NUT) by writing to them at Hamilton House, Mabledon Place, London WC1H 9BD. (b) You can get membership at a lower rate of various bodies such as the Institute of Electronic Engineering and the British Film Institute. Always ask if an association gives concessions to students.

Social Security. You are not entitled to Unemployment Benefit at any time you are on a full-time course of education. You can't usually get Income Support, either, because you are not regarded as available for full-time work. But if you are a lone parent bringing up a child under 16, or if you are disabled or deaf, you may be able to get Income Support while you're on your course. Ask about this at the Social Security office.

If you have a partner who is also a student, and you are bringing up a child, you may be able to get Income Support if you can't get a job during the summer vacation and are available, willing and able to work.

Housing Benefit. If you are a full-time student you can claim Housing Benefit if you are:
- a lone parent;
- one of a couple (both full-time students) with dependent children;
- solely responsible for a child boarded out with you by a local authority or voluntary organization;
- disabled;
- getting Income Support.

National Health Service charges. If you get Income Support, you and your dependants will also get free NHS prescriptions, sight tests, dental treatment, vouchers for glasses, wigs and fabric supports, and refunds of your travel costs to and from hospital for NHS treatment.

If you get pregnant while you are a full-time student you will get free NHS prescriptions and dental treatment while you're pregnant and for a year after your baby is born (as does every pregnant woman).

Get leaflet FB23 from a Post Office for full information on social security for students.

A cautionary note about National Insurance (NI) contributions
Full-time students do *not* have to pay NI contributions, but they *may* pay the non-employed contribution if they want to. Your LEA grant will not make provision for this, however.

If you have been in a job and paying NI contributions before you became a student, non-payment when you are a student will result in a gap in your contribution record and this will affect entitlement to long-term benefits such as retirement pension, the grant payable if you have a baby, and death grant.

NI contributions are very expensive, and few older students who are relying on grants for support feel they can afford this protection. If you really need advice about whether to contribute, see your local office of the DSS (address in telephone directory). Contributions can be paid up later, if you wish; and since the scheme is based on an average of 50 weekly payments a year, you can make up one year's pension contribution in 25 years' work!

If you take a paid job during your vacations from college, you will have to pay the normal contributions.

What is the easiest way to get money to study?

It will be clear by now that if, as a mature student, you want to get financial help, you would get it most easily by becoming a *full-time* student on a degree-level course, or some other high-level course such as HND or Dip.HE. The other main route is to take a course under the Employment Training Scheme.

Career Development Loans

The Department of Employment, in conjunction with Barclays, Clydesdale and the Co-operative banks, offer Career Development Loans to help you pay for vocational training in a wide range of subjects in the professional, managerial, scientific and technical fields. You can apply for a CDL of between £300 and £5,000 to help cover 80% of course fees plus the full cost of books and materials, and living expenses where appropriate. No repayments are required during the training period and for up to three months afterwards. During this time the DoE pays the interest on your loan. At the end of this period, when your new skills have hopefully led to a better job, it is up to you to repay the loan and any further interest over a period agreed in advance – usually three to five years.

Anyone over 18 – whether employed or unemployed – who lives or intends to train in Great Britain, can apply for such a loan, as long as she is taking a course that:

- is vocational, i.e. job-related (though not necessarily related to your previous occupation);
- lasts at least a week and no more than a year;
- is not supported financially by an employer or a full mandatory or discretionary grant/award by the local education authority.

Note, however, that your unemployment benefit money could be affected if your training prevents you from being available for work.

Tax relief for vocational training

From April 1992 you can get tax relief on the payments you make for your own vocational training which can lead to the National Vocational Qualification (NVQ) or a Scottish Vocational Qualification (SVQ) up to and including level 4. These are qualifications accredited by the National Council for Vocational Qualifications. You can get relief for any part of the training, even if you are not studying for a full qualification.

You can get this tax relief if you are resident in the UK for tax purposes and you are *not* receiving financial assistance for a course under any government scheme. Relief does not extend to general educational qualifications such as GCSEs or A levels

(Standard Grades and Highers in Scotland).

In practice, the system discriminates against older students if they cannot study full-time. Yet a majority of women returning to education prefer part-time day courses, because they fit in with their domestic responsibilities. But these courses are subject to the vagaries of the discretionary grants system, and are becoming harder to get.

If you think that you couldn't possibly contemplate full-time study, don't lose heart. Much of this book is looking at ways in which you could manage very well. All you need is a lot of help and some good planning. So read on!

Chapter 6
Fitting in at college

Will you feel out of place?

How will you feel when you have to spend a substantial part of your time at college? If you are taking a single evening class, you won't feel so involved in college life. But if you are spending a lot of time there you will want to feel that you fit in.

Lack of awareness of how colleges function often leaves students frustrated and angry. You may not know precisely what to expect from college life, but you probably think the main function of the teaching staff is to teach and look after students. But the staff may believe that college-level students should learn by themselves (not expecting to be spoon-fed) and that if students don't learn it is because they are poor students. Now, bear in mind that very few teachers outside schools have been trained to *teach*. So spare some sympathy for their problem when dealing with students as old as, or older than themselves, some of whom need to be guided through basic study skills, and others who have considerably more experience of, say, trade unions, party politics, working in industry, or educating children by raising them.

A college can seem like a foreign land when you first arrive there. So make an effort to understand its rules, customs and habits. There will be set rules and also unwritten rules which are not known to outsiders. You need to make yourself an insider by knowing the social rules, the gossip, the politics. If the students have written an alternative prospectus to the college, get hold of it for candid comments on staff, lecture styles, courses, amenities.

The type of course you are taking will govern the demands and level of work expected of you. If you take a course which is specially set up for adults, you stand a good chance of settling down quickly. As I said in an earlier chapter, women on Wider Opportunities for Women courses (job training) seem to develop

It's never too late ...

strong group identity and provide good support for each other, apparently. And tutors running courses in basic study skills, or as groundwork for higher education, know that they must not rush along faster than the student can follow. If a college is really trying to make it easier for older women with family commitments to study, the lecturers will be experienced in teaching adults, the lecture times will be set for convenient times for them, and there will probably be childcare facilities. On courses like these you need have no fear that you will be out of place, and you can find such courses in universities, colleges of adult education, and further education colleges.

However, if you go on to a GCSE and A level course at a college of further education, or perhaps at a school, you may find all the teaching geared to young people of 16 and 18, and teachers with little time or inclination to make special provision for an older student. You have to know well what you are doing, in order to fit in here. But many women do exactly this, and are very successful in their exam results.

Advanced level work at a college will usually require you to work much more on your own, and this shift from elementary work where you get a lot of help can be traumatic. But it is part of a necessary process if you want to aim higher and go on to degree work.

The adjustment to being a student at a university on a degree course, is probably the most difficult for you to make, though I remind you that thousands of women *have done it successfully*. You will soon discover that universities are not necessarily relaxed, unworldly places. Academics are usually busy people, often worried about their research, on which promotion depends. They may be swamped by administrative and committee work, and regard students as a necessary nuisance; indeed, they may want no more contact with students than the minimum (giving lectures and marking essays). But many members of staff care deeply about students, and make a tremendous effort to be available for help and advice. Find out who are the helpful teachers early on; ask other students, and also the departmental secretaries who can be mines of information.

At a large university, you may be shocked to find yourself in a class of several hundred students for a popular lecture course, and wonder how on earth to get individual attention if you need it. The answer is that most British universities arrange some small-group teaching, but you must also be prepared to bang on doors for help if you are in real difficulties. Few academics have ever had real difficulty themselves with academic work, so they often *cannot* understand a student's difficulties. This may show a lack of imagination on their part, but it is better for you to keep on asking for help than to get angry and resentful. For example, if you have worked hard, read widely and thought long about an essay, and then you get a low mark for it, pluck up the courage to go and see the person who marked it. Ask, on the basis of wanting to do better next time, what you failed to take into account and the criteria being used for marking. A lot of intellectual work is a kind of game, a playing with ideas and language, and you may need to know the rules of the game before you can play it properly.

Some general problems can arise from being a *woman* student. You may imagine that academics are infinitely more fair-minded than other people, and will *not* be prejudiced against women. But they are just as likely to believe that women are naturally inferior, and to cite female failings to prove their point. Most teachers would say they make absolutely no distinction between male and female students, as far as work is concerned, but you can get clues to their attitudes from the jokes they make during lectures, or their generalizations about the way women think and behave. Some of them may talk about women's lack of interest in theoretical issues, conveniently overlooking their own responsibility to make these issues comprehensible. And the view that women are not up to the rigours of academic work can be self-validating: if they begin to believe it, so appearing to prove they are less academically talented than men. The only way to deal with this is to believe in yourself and the example of other women who are making names for themselves in the academic world.

Another problem that many women students report is the difficulty of taking part in class discussions when there are a lot of men students who are more confident of their opinions. You may think you will have little useful to contribute, but you may also find it difficult to get a word in, or to have your ideas taken seriously when you do. I don't think men are always aware they are doing this, but it is a phenomenon most women recognize. To deal with it you can write down before seminars a few points you want to make, or questions you want to ask, and this will give you confidence to speak up freely. You could then open up the discussion, instead of waiting for someone else to do it, and thus ensure that your ideas were discussed. You could also make friends outside the classroom with some of the men students in the seminar group, and then it is less likely they will totally exclude you.

A further problem for older women students is that some lecturers are not prepared to make allowance for your domestic responsibilities. They may indicate that if you can't manage your domestic problems, you are a dilettante without serious purpose. Now, this can be very annoying if the same teachers (women as well as men) are sympathetic to young students who fall behind in their work because of emotional problems concerning unhappy love affairs. You can only point out, gently but firmly, that only the most unusual of pressures (not the day to day ones) makes you ask for special treatment such as an extension of time to complete an essay. Emphasize that normally you give priority to study.

There is no easy way to deal with these problems. A good tip is to find out early how your lecturer or tutor regards older women students, and if there is any real hostility, try to change courses or tutors.

It can be a major shock for older students to be pitchforked into the impersonal world of a university geared to 18 to 21 year olds. But one of the nicest surprises about going to college when you are older is finding out how friendly the young students can be. They are usually suffering (like you) from feelings of being transplanted into alien soil. They won't question why you are a student (not always knowing why they are at college, either!). They have fellow feelings about work loads and how to discipline themselves to study on their own (these youngsters have been used to having school teachers and parents breathing down their necks, and find it hard to decide for themselves how much to do). If you make the effort to talk to them, young students will be helpful, friendly and responsive. Don't intimidate them by stressing your life experience and achievements: show them that you too have a lot to learn. They will make you feel younger by accepting you as one of them, and they will boost your confidence by telling you they think you are *great* to be doing the course. Learn from them, too, not to take things so seriously that you miss out on the *fun* of being a student.

Life after class

There's a lot more to being a student than just going to lectures and seminars, writing essays and doing exams. Research into the way students respond to their years as undergraduates shows that the ones who get deeply involved with college or university life, taking part in social, sporting or political activities, seem to gain immeasurably from their education compared with those who keep themselves to themselves and concentrate only on academic work. So you should aim both to make friends at a personal level, with other students and members of staff who are friendly, and to join in some group activities.

Meeting people

Talking and listening is the basis of social life at college. You will find that most students, of all ages, desperately want to talk about both academic and personal problems. After all, teachers and tutors have little time to listen to student worries unless they are really serious ones. Young people are often homesick, but don't want to admit it, and they frequently have problems learning to live independently. Mature students worry about things that young people frequently shrug off, and here you will find that comparing notes with other older students is a great help. If you are willing to talk to other students, you will have no difficulty getting on with them. Talk to anyone you happen to sit by in a lecture or seminar, to stand by in a corridor, or sit by in refectory. Suggest that a group of students from your class meets for coffee or lunch together sometimes. Invite students you like to visit your home and family. If you are an ordinarily friendly person, you will find plenty of people willing to talk, and you can learn a lot from them.

It's never too late ...

Getting to know staff can be more difficult, and it depends how interested they are in forming links with students. But you can always stay behind after a lecture or seminar to ask a question. You can make an appointment with a lecturer to discuss a particular worry. And you can suggest to other students that you jointly invite a lecturer or tutor to join you all for coffee or a drink after class.

Joining in

You probably think that if you go to college as a mature woman with family responsibilities, you won't have time or energy to take part in any social life at college. But once you get there, and realize how much is going on, I think you will find facilities you can't resist. However busy you are, there are times when you could go for a swim, take up jogging, play squash, badminton or tennis, or do yoga, keep-fit or popmobility. And you are sure to want to join some of the student societies.

Most colleges have a student union. Generally speaking, you *have* to belong to it, but your membership fee is paid by the LEA, direct to the college, along with the tuition fees. So you are entitled to use all the facilities provided by the student union, and to go to all meetings. The individual student clubs and societies charge a small extra fee which you pay yourself.

For you, as an older student, the priority would be to join the Mature Students Union (MSU) if there is a branch at your college. Non-politically aligned, it exists to introduce older students to each other by arranging social events, and to advise and assist you with welfare and academic problems you might meet as a mature person. It also works with the National Union of Students (NUS) to pass on the views of older students to the government. For example, in the past MSU has campaigned for college nursery facilities, higher grants for dependants, and to try (unsuccessfully) to get older students credits for National Insurance. They are keen on expanding the number of mature students, especially women students. So, if there isn't an MSU at your college, try to get one started. For advice, contact Margaret Devine, Secretary, Mature Students' Society, c/o 6 Salisbury Road, Harrow, Middlesex HA1 1MY.

As a woman, you might also want to get involved in women's

rights issues (such as shelters for battered wives, the rape crisis centre, improved maternity services). There may be a Women's Centre at your college, but if not there is almost certain to be one in the local town. Either would welcome your interest and support.

There are student clubs, in colleges around the country, to cover every interest from potholing or skydiving to eastern mysticism or stamp-collecting (and you can always start one of your own). Joining a club is easy – just pay your membership fee and turn up for meetings. Some clubs meet at lunchtimes or in the late afternoon, others in the evenings. The sports facilities are usually available all day and evening, and at weekends too, so you could take your family along to enjoy them. 'Sport for All' has successfully encouraged local townspeople to use college sports facilities, usually for a fee.

The choice of student clubs is so varied that it is difficult to do more than catalogue them in groups:

Societies connected with study
There are usually clubs for each subject taught in college, e.g. Archaeology, Physics, Forestry, Philosophy. They invite speakers, and it is surprising what big names they can attract – people seem to love talking to students. They arrange outings and social events. You will meet both students and staff in these clubs.

Ethnic societies
Each group from the UK and overseas seems to run a club, and it isn't all talk and campaigns. There are social evenings when the food and drink of the country is provided, and people sing their own songs and do their own folk dances. But they welcome anyone interested in learning about their culture.

Religious groups
All the major religions and many less well-known ones are represented in most universities and colleges.

Political societies
In common with other student societies, the party political societies (Labour, Liberal Democrat, Conservative, etc.) attract big

names to speak to them. Politicians expect students to be the leaders of the future, so ex-Cabinet Ministers and party chairmen come along to explain their policies, and the meetings are usually very lively because students are notoriously irreverent where public figures are concerned.

Pressure groups
These are societies to support all sorts of campaigns and causes such as, for example, Anti-Nuclear, Conservation, Hunt Saboteurs.

Community Action groups (CA)
This is the sort of student activity not usually noticed, because it does not make the newspaper headlines. It is an attempt to bridge the gap between the college and the local townspeople. As a mature student, you may not be quite sure which group you really belong to, so joining CA groups could be just the thing for you. CA work can take the form of putting on plays or concerts in Old People's Homes, or for local children and youth clubs. It can involve sporting events, such as running a local children's team or helping coach disabled people. A lot of CA work is fun rather than hard work.

CA also runs regular projects such as teaching English to immigrants, helping run youth clubs, visiting local pensioners and the housebound, as well as gardening and decorating jobs and help with the local Women's Refuge.

Supporting CA projects is a good way to get to know young students and an excellent way to learn how politics affects people (if you are the sort of person who dislikes political parties and political arguments about principles). You will soon find out how society treats its minorities, and the way cuts in public spending affect ordinary people.

Student Rags
Student Rag weeks are what people make them, but they provide a good way for you to work with younger students to raise money for local good causes. Some students believe that the work done by charities should be carried out by the State, and they choose not to absolve the State of its responsibilities by raising money for

charity. But we don't live in a society in which the State *does* take all such responsibility, and meanwhile the problems of the old, sick, infirm, disabled, etc. are very much with us, and you may therefore want to do what you can to help these charities.

Rag Weeks need a lot of organization, and if you have experience of committee and fund-raising work you could be very valuable. You could probably approach the relevant bodies with more confidence – the police, local council, St. John's Ambulance, local shopkeepers etc. You might even have local links which could get help and publicity for the events. The nice thing about Rag Week is that it involves students of all ages, and assists links with the local community.

One last point: as a mature woman student you might be able to get changes made in those really awful Rag Mags which seem to consist of dreadful jokes at the expense of women!

Music groups
There is often an amateur orchestra that would welcome you if you play an instrument. You could sing in a choir, or join a Gilbert and Sullivan society. Jazz groups are popular.

Drama groups
They are always glad to welcome older students with experience of acting, or who will help with scenery and costumes. This is a very good way to mix with younger students.

Film Societies
Ever popular because it gives you a chance to see golden oldies and foreign classics, as well as up-to-date films which have not been commercially popular.

Get-up-and-go groups
The variety of sports facilities will depend on the size and resources of your college, of course. But you may be able to choose swimming, keep-fit, yoga, popmobility, athletics, fencing, squash, badminton, tennis etc. And there may be ballroom dancing or folk dancing. You will probably be able to take your husband, partner or children along to many of these activities.

Off-site you could probably go in for rock-climbing, exploring underground caves, fell-walking, canoeing or sailing.

Your age and general fitness are bound to have some effect on the kind of activities you can do. If you are over 40 and want to take ballet lessons, you are not going to become a prima ballerina, but the exercises are splendid if you have the stamina for them.

For the less energetic
Pop concerts, discos, or just propping up the bar may suit you better, with the odd game of darts or bar billiards for exercise!

Getting more involved

At college level

Student Union Officer. Women now form 40 % of the total number of students, yet most of the student unions have few women on their executives. Women don't come forward for the posts: the thought of speaking at the hustings seems to intimidate them, though they may be fine on a one-to-one basis. This reluctance is not altogether surprising, since there have been well-publicized cases of men students ridiculing their female colleagues at union meetings and conferences.

But students bodies *do* have women officers, and they don't want to frighten women away, so if you want to take part in union affairs you will be welcome. If they hold meetings at times difficult for you, ask them to have them at other times. And also try to persuade them to lay on some training sessions in public speaking which might help women gain more confidence in airing their opinions.

Student representatives on governing bodies. In most colleges, students have some say, via staff-student committees or places on governing bodies, in how the college is run. Your student representatives might have to be reminded from time to time that they represent *all* students, not just themselves or their own age-group. But you could come forward and stand for election, too. A lot of mature students have been prominent in college government, and their experience has been a useful counterbalance to their younger colleagues.

At national level: the National Union of Students (NUS)
NUS is the second largest youth movement in the country – second to the Girl Guides. It is a very large organization with a million members in universities and colleges of higher education and further education.

But NUS is not only for young people: its members range in age from 16 to 60. It is increasingly interested in the needs of mature students, and since it is a powerful, well-organized group working for *all* students, it can be of great assistance to you. It is passionately in favour of an open system of education for all, and is always willing to give advice and help to non-traditional students like you. If your college union is affiliated to the NUS (and most are) then you are automatically a member. If it is not, you could ask the NUS at 461 Holloway Road, London N7 6LJ whether it would be possible to join as an individual member.

The chief role of NUS is to provide information and help for college student unions, and to represent their views to local education authorities, the government and other national bodies. The benefits of membership to you as an individual may not immediately be clear. But the information your local union gives you probably comes from NUS, particularly on grants, education and welfare, social security, income tax, housing, contraception, etc. NUS also runs a Publications Department, which issues the newspaper *National Student* (found on most campuses but you can write to NUS headquarters for a copy). And of course they run many policy conferences, which representatives of affiliated college unions attend.

As I said earlier, NUS is very interested in mature students, and welcomes older students representing local unions or mature Student Unions. Individual benefits of belonging to NUS are:

legal advice from their Legal Department;
a green International Student card (ISIC card) which gives you discounts all over the world;
NUS Marketing (a discount card which you can use in listed stores and mail order services);

the newspaper National Student;
occasional events such as big disco roadshows.

Note if you are a part-time student

If you are a part-time student, you may not really see yourself as a student at all. And I'm afraid most student unions, for their part, ignore part-time students and their problems. But the student union *should* be there to help you, as it does other students, regardless of how many hours a week you study. If you belong to the student union at your college, you can get the benefits of NUS membership if that union is affiliated to NUS.

NUS holds a special National Part-Time Student Conference annually, to discuss issues affecting part-timers. Make sure your student union sends someone (and why not you?) to that conference to speak for you.

NUS Women's Campaign

Not affiliated to any political grouping, this is open to all members of NUS. It concerns itself with women's issues such as attacks on women on campuses, discrimination against women in education; and also general issues such as contraception, abortion and nursery facilities.

If the NUS Women's Campaign is unheard of in your college, you might like to start a group. Contact NUS Headquarters in London (461 Holloway Road, N7 6LJ – tel. (071) 272 8900) for information and to get on to their mailing list. They have a lot of useful tips on how to set up a group.

Chapter 7
Getting down to study

You cannot hope to master more than a fraction of the existing 'stock of knowledge' at any level of education. But your aim should not be total coverage: it should be to find out more, to understand more, to create. Your natural curiosity about the questions that remain to be answered will hopefully lead you on to a lifetime of further learning.

Learning, which is the process of being educated, involves a set of skills which can be practised and developed. *Studying*, which is an active effort at learning, is only successful if you learn well and efficiently. There is no obvious reason why mature women students like you should have greater study problems than other students (though you may lack confidence because you have been away from school for a long time), but the following ideas would help you:

Find a good place to study (a room of your own) and equip it as a working area;

Learn to take, keep and use good notes;

Learn to read rapidly and with understanding;

Learn to present reports on practical work concisely;

Learn to write essays.

All these things are easier said than done. You may, of course, be one of the lucky people who have already learned these habits, or picked them up from teachers or friends. But most people are not so fortunate. This chapter deals in part with ways of developing study skills on your own, but of course you could go to actual Study Skills classes of the kind described in Chapter 3 and get more formal instruction. Either way, remember that academic success is clearly related to organized study habits.

It's never too late ...

A good place to study

If you are going to study at home for several hours a day, or even a couple of times a week, you need a place to work that you can call your own (even if it has to be your bedroom). Use the same place each time, so that you associate it with study and can leave opened books and papers there.

Choose somewhere fairly quiet that will not be occupied by other members of your family when you want to work. You can't expect your family to keep quiet all the time, so invest in earplugs, or wear earphones and listen to soft music which excludes the house noises.

Choose a room with plenty of light, and a comfortable temperature. If it is too hot or too cold, your mind will be distracted by a sweaty brow or frozen feet. If it is not well ventilated, it will get stuffy and you will develop a headache or fall asleep.

You need certain items of equipment, such as:

A desk. This should be sturdy and comfortable to use. It could be a table, or a piece of wood placed on two small chests of drawers. Make sure it is at a height you find comfortable. Keep on it containers for paper, pens, paper-clips, and card references.

A desk chair. Claim a chair for your own use in your study place, so that you are not always looking for something to sit on.

A desk lamp. Make sure you have adequate lighting and that you can move the lamp around to wherever you are sitting (a long piece of flex helps).

A filing system. Everything mentioned below can be obtained from a good stationer.

(a) *Loose-leaf ring binders*: Almost certainly you will wish to file the bulk of your notes by subject. One of the best schemes is a loose-leaf ring binder, which has a lot of advantages:
- you can add fresh notes at any time and in any sequence that suits you; use wide-lined paper so that you have space between the lines for additions or corrections;

Getting down to study

- you can sub-divide the material by using coloured cardboard dividers;
- you can expand endlessly into other folders, if this becomes necessary;
- you can re-organize your material quickly, at any time you need to.

The best way to use a loose-leaf system is to *write on one side* of the paper only, and start new topics on new sheets of paper. In this way you can remove sheets and move them around, without upsetting notes on other topics.

(b) *Cardboard folders*. The loose-leaf system may not be so useful if you want to keep a lot of pamphlets, maps, diagrams, or press cuttings, in addition to your notes. In this case, you need a series of large cardboard folders, of the kind designed for filing cabinets. If you haven't got a filing cabinet to keep them in, use a large cardboard box from the grocer's.

(c) *Card files*. For small items of information, quick references, and revision purposes, it is useful to have a card index. Like the loose-leaf binder, it is quickly added to, amended, or re-ordered. The standard size of index card is 5" by 3", but for handwritten notes the large sizes may be more useful, say 6" by 4" or 8" by 5". You can keep cards in a special card index box or use a small cardboard box.

The following are not essential but will make your work easier:

A typewriter. A small secondhand portable would be a good investment. Typewritten essays and projects save embarrassment over handwriting, and are a boon to those who read your work. You can also type up lecture notes and reduce the amount of paper you store.

A bookcase. Keep your most frequently-used books near your working desk and have references at your finger tips.

A telephone. A telephone in your room can be both a blessing and a curse. It is good not to have a dash downstairs to take a wrong number call. The children can let you know if they are going to be late home from school. And you can consult fellow-students if you have a problem.

But you don't want to have long chats with friends when you are busy. So learn how to terminate a phone conversation politely. And put a sign on the phone, saying, "Am I talking too long?" If you know you waste time that way.

Learn to take, keep and use good notes

What are notes for? To help your memory, of course. You can't hope permanently to remember details of a lecture, a book or a discussion, so you need to write down the most important items and use them for reference and revision. The notes have to be arranged to suit yourself, because it is *your* memory and understanding that concerns you. Note-taking helps you concentrate, and as you write you become more involved in the learning process than you would if you just kept on listening or reading.

What are good notes? There are no hard-and-fast rules because notes are such a personal aid, but all notes need to be as follows:

Concise – if the notes are too long, it will be a boring job to look though them, so you probably won't bother at all.

Clear – you simply must make notes that you can understand immediately you re-read them. If you can't read them quickly and thus refresh your memory, they are no use to you at all.

Written in your own words – using your own language ensures that you put down what you have understood, and nothing else.

Taking notes from a book

- This may sound an obvious point, but don't forget to start by making a note of the title of the book and the author's name! If you expect to refer to it in a formal paper or dissertation, take down the publisher, and the place and date of publication, as well.
- You are not aiming to précis the whole book, so try to record

the main topics covered and the important supporting evidence. Where an elaborate argument is mounted, you need to make a note of each step in the argument, expressed in your own words. It may be true that the author expresses his or her ideas more elegantly than you ever could, but don't copy word for word.
- Take each chapter in turn and itemize: (i) the main topic; (ii) the arguments and illustrations or evidence; (iii) the results or conclusions of the chapter.
- If you want to make direct quotations, keep them short and don't forget the page number. Finding a quotation later can be frustrating and time-wasting.

Taking notes at lectures

Learn to listen properly

Listening intently involves a lot more than just keeping quiet. It involves trying to understand what people are *really* saying, without dismissing their ideas out of hand because you don't agree with them. This kind of listening is an art, and it is rare, but it is a good art to cultivate.

Women who have grown used to doing several things at once, attending to the needs of several people, seem to find it difficult to concentrate on one thing to the exclusion of others. So when they go back to the classroom or lecture theatre, they have to force themselves to put out of mind the practical problems that beset them. It requires a big effort to push out of your mind, as inappropriate *at that moment* what the family will have for supper, or whether your child will remember a dental appointment. But if you don't do so, you will not follow the arguments, and you might as well not be at the lecture.

If you find that your attention has been wandering, ask a fellow student at the end of the lecture whether you have understood correctly, giving a swift review of what you think the lecturer was saying. Or go and see the lecturer if you are really adrift. Of course, some lectures are just awful – boring and difficult to follow – so it may not be wholly your fault if your attention has wandered. But not all boring lectures are useless. The lecturer may have something important to say in spite of a boring manner of presentation. Only if you learn to listen properly can you tell what is worth listening to.

Write down the meaningful ideas and facts in note form
- Don't make a transcript – that is, don't try to get down everything that is said.
- Your notes will depend on the shape of the lecture. In science lectures more notes may be necessary, where the precise details of apparatus, experiment, results or mathematical proofs or formulae have to be remembered, but inevitably the lecturer will realize that you need time to take down such details, or s/he may have anticipated the problem and provided duplicated hand-outs.
- A good lecturer will tell you at the beginning of the lecture what s/he is going to cover. At that point you write these points down under each other, at the top of the page:
X
Y
Z
- Then put 1.X and wait for the main points to be made, jotting them down underneath. Follow with 2.Y and 3.Z. The lecturer will usually emphasize the key points by telling you what is important or by using a tone of voice which implies significance. You may not always agree with the lecturer about the relative significance of a point, but just follow at this stage the way s/he communicates the logical structure of the topic and the important points to note. You can argue about them later.
- The lecturer may also finish by summarizing the points s/he wants you to remember, and by providing you with advance notice of what s/he will deal with in the following lectures. Now, students often take the words, "Next time we shall be dealing with ..." as being the signal to close their notebooks and start rushing for the door. But knowing what to expect next time may be important in alerting you to the logical structure of the course, as well as suggesting what you might read or think about for next time. So it is worth staying to hear what is being said.
- You need not make particularly neat notes in class, if you intend to copy them up later and put them into your own

words. So write short sentences, and use shorthand, symbols, abbreviations, slang, etc. to make note-taking easier. Arrows can be used to connect thoughts and statements, replacing word explanations. Everyone uses arrows in the sciences, but you can use them for any subject. Other effective symbols and abbreviations used in all subjects are as follows:

+	plus, positive	w/	with
−	minus, negative	w/i	within
↑	increase, higher	w/o	without
↓	decrease, lower	wh/	which
=	equal	4	for
=ly	equally	∴	therefore
<	less than	∵	because
<	greater than	info	information
∞	infinity	c.	approxi-
e.g.	for example	approx.	mately
wrt	with respect to	re	reference (or with reference to)
avg	average		

- You can also make up your own abbreviations. For example, if building materials is mentioned once, you write it in long form and put b.m. in brackets, using the shortened form thereafter in the notes.
- Your job is not finished until you have looked over your notes carefully, and this should be done soon after the lecture, while you can still decipher your jottings and remember the points the lecturer was making. If you have missed important names or terms, check up with a friend or consult a textbook. Write a brief synopsis of the lecture, in your own words, forcing yourself to review what was said. If you think of questions you would have liked to ask, or come up with an idea you would like to discuss, write it down under your notes and bring it up when you get the opportunity. Such summaries and questions will be useful for revising, and also for ideas in essays.

It's never too late ...

Learn to read rapidly and with understanding

As one lecturer told a first-year class of students, "You go to university to *read* for a degree, so do as much reading as you can." "What are you reading?", addressed to a British student, means, "What subject are you studying?" Only in the hard sciences are you likely to be given a basic textbook. Arts, humanities and social science students will get lists of dozens of recommended books for reading. So the ability to read rapidly, and with understanding, is a great help to any student.

How well do *you* read? You have probably been reading since you were about 5 years old, and for many years have read newspapers, magazines and books for a couple of hours a day or so. But as a student you will have to read a lot more than that: you need to read fast, and to comprehend what you read. If you can't do this, it may be because you have a faulty reading habit such as one of the following.

Do you move your lips or read aloud as you read? If you do, you should put your hand tightly over your mouth as you read, to stop your lips moving, and try to read so rapidly that there isn't time to move your lips. Practice on material which is not difficult to understand. The reason for a fault like this is that you may have first learned to read out loud, and are now going through the same motions without making any noise.

Are you a word-by-word reader? This means that you can't read fast because you pause for every word on the line, and constantly retrace your steps. Do your eyes get part way down the page and then more back a few words or lines? Do your eyes wander aimlessly back and forth, trying to understand what you have read? If so, you need to learn to take in at a glance an average of two words or more. Don't dally over words, or retrace your steps as a general rule. Of course, there are times when even the best reader has to go back and check what she read earlier, but good readers do little of this. Reading quickly enables you to move on fast enough not to forget by the end of the sentence what was said at the beginning! So faster reading helps you understand the salient ideas. Here are two simple suggestions for increasing your reading speed and understanding:

1. Move your index finger along the line you are reading: keep going line after line, without hesitating. If your eyes are moving faster than your finger, move your finger faster and faster until you are really skimming along.

2. Always use your finger as a guide to what you are reading if you tend to be a daydreamer and to be easily distracted.

Are you frequently stopped by an unfamiliar word? If so, increase your vocabulary by using a dictionary. Look for the ideas behind the words, even if you are not sure of the precise meaning of a particular word. Use small index cards on which you can write words, and underneath put a definition and a phrase showing how to use it. Definitions shift, of course – such is the glory of language – and you have to be sensitive to these changes.

Bear in mind the differences between *general words* which you will find in literature and history, to describe and interpret things of general interest, and the *jargon or technical words* which may have meanings very different from the common sense ones, to express concepts, laws or special meanings in a particular subject. A book may contain a *glossary* or dictionary of important terms used, or might give an extended discussion of what the word means in the text. Elementary textbooks in the subject often give good definitions of words, and there are specialized dictionaries for technical subjects such as physics and engineering (which you can find in libraries or buy as paperbacks).

Skimming or scanning

If at present you read everything at the same rate, you will need as a student to learn to *vary* your speed of reading, according to what you are trying to get out of the material. This is because you will get a long list of 'suggested reading' in every subject you study, apart from the hard sciences where a few textbooks are recommended. And mature students are notorious for taking their work very seriously, often to the point of assuming that they should try to read everything on the list (which leads to too much reading and not enough thinking). Articles can be read fairly quickly, so don't usually present a great problem, but it is difficult for a new student to decide which of the suggested books are more important, if no special guidance is given. So you need to be able to work quickly through books, to find out what ideas are being propounded in them. You don't want to sacrifice understanding to speed, and you should not just plod through the material in a dogged sort of way, feeling nothing but relief when it is all over. What you *can* do is:

- Look at the Contents page first. Do the chapter headings present a basic argument? This will give you a clear picture of the shape of the book.
- See if you can get an idea of the book from the Introduction, but avoid ploughing through long, convoluted Introductions if you find they are confusing you.
- Always look at the Conclusion or Summary chapter at the end, if there is one (don't be afraid of spoiling your enjoyment!).
- If you are looking for information which is clearly contained in one or two chapters, go straight to them and don't be afraid to skip others.
- But if you want the gist of the whole book, deal with each chapter in turn.
- Taking the chapter, if the book is reasonably well written each chapter should be organized into some logical form. It, too, may have a beginning, a middle and an end, so it is worth looking at the first and last paragraphs to see what it is about. The chapter may be in continuous prose or have subheadings. Within each subsection the prose will be divided into paragraphs. Schools used to teach that each paragraph should contain one idea, and it isn't a bad rule of thumb to expect to find an idea, or the development of an idea that has gone before. When looking at individual paragraphs, however, beware of thinking that the main idea is contained in the first sentence. This is not always the case, as the first sentence may be a linking one to the last paragraph. So try and spot words like 'but' and 'however' cropping up halfway through the paragraph to lead to the main idea.
- There will always be certain paragraphs that require very serious attention, and you must remember that you can't skim and scan over everything.
- At the end of your reading, ask yourself, "What have I learned

from reading this?" Compare what the book says with what other people have written on the subject, and also with what *you* think and believe. Look for the author's evidence to support controversial views. If you think the author's interpretation is wrong, what evidence could you offer to refute it? Ask yourself whether the author has an axe to grind, and look for loaded words designed to evoke emotional rather than logical conclusions. If you keep a critical state of mind as you read, you will learn to think for yourself and not merely soak up other people's opinions. The more you learn, the more you will criticize the arguments of others, until one day perhaps you will come up with a brilliant idea of your own!

Learn to present reports concisely

In science and certain social sciences, practical work forms an important part of your studies. To understand the scientific processes discussed in lectures it is essential to develop a 'feel' for the way in which scientists investigate problems. It is this insight into experimental work, as much as the skills developed in handling apparatus, which makes practicals so important.

Reports on practical work usually underline the research strategy adopted, as well as recording the results obtained. It is also necessary in some reports to relate the practical work to theoretical ideas which underlie the experiment. In science, 'practicals' and 'theory' cannot be separated into neat compartments, since both are part of the process of understanding.

There is a tendency for students to spend far too long in writing detailed and excessively elaborate reports. However, a useful tip is to attempt a short abstract at the end of writing an experimental report. This should be a few sentences covering (a) the reason for doing the experiment; (b) some idea of the results and whether or not it was a success; (c) a brief conclusion. You would always have to do this in any industrial report, i.e. a report for a company, so it is a useful exercise for the future.

Remember that there is a good deal of thinking and reading to be done, and that report writing should occupy only a minority of your time.

It's never too late ...

Learn to write essays

What is the point of essays? Well, *essayer* is the French for 'to try', and essays are only attempts or tries, rather than polished statements for publication. At college level they give you practice in organized, creative thinking and writing about a subject, going beyond a mere recital of facts. Your teacher sees what you are learning and understanding, and essays are excellent practice for later exams, project reports and dissertations.

Whatever your subject, you will probably find that you have to write in essay form at some time. In arts and social sciences this might mean something short every week; as a medical student you might have to write a long social psychology project once in five years; but whenever you do it you will have to learn to present material logically.

If you hate writing essays, you will find that many students of all ages share your feelings, so it is not a problem for you alone. You can discuss essays with other students, as an important method of learning and clarifying ideas. But don't copy anyone else's work, or allow anyone to copy from yours. Plagiarism is a grievous sin at college.

Beginning your essay: look at the question

Difficulties start if you don't define the terms of the question and work out exactly what is required. Different questions require different sorts of answers, so look at the precise wording and think what it means. Are you being asked for a broad outline or a detailed account? Are you asked to refer to particular sources of information or experimental data? In short, what kind of essay are you being asked to write. Your guide is entirely in the essay question, and it is a good idea to show that you understand the question by re-phrasing it in your first paragraph.

Some of the terms frequently used in questions are as follows. Make sure you are clear about the precise meaning of each term.

Compare: look at the similarities and differences between, say, two or more objects, people or policies.
Contrast: point out clearly the differences between objects,

people or policies.

Criticize: pass judgement on the merits, as well as the defects; back your opinions by discussing the evidence.

Define: give the clear meaning of; mark the limits of; describe in exact terms (there may be a number of definitions).

Discuss: argue the case for and against; give reasons for each side of the discussion; write about in detail; and come to some sort of conclusion if you can.

Describe: give a detailed account of; trace the form of.

Differentiate between: recognize, define and show that you understand the difference between.

Distinguish between: mark the significant differences between; perceive distinctly.

Evaluate: find the value of; make an appraisal of (on the basis of its truth or usefulness).

Explain: make plain, clear or intelligible; account for; give reasons for.

Illustrate: explain by way of example.

Interpret: explain the meaning of, in your own words; assign significance to.

Justify: show to be true; right or reasonable; give adequate grounds for your proof or exoneration; answer the main objections.

Narrate: give a step-by-step sequence of events.

Outline: give a brief, general explanation or summary; emphasize the structure without too much detail.

Relate: establish the connections between; show how things affect each other.

State: expound plainly and in detail.

Summarize: make a brief statement of the essential points: précis.

Collecting material for an essay

When you have decided what type of essay you are going to write, and what its scope will be, you will have to do some research into the subject matter. It is no use getting hold of a lot of books and reading them all, hoping that something useful will come up. It is better to work out some specific questions you want to answer. The essay title will probably break down into several parts, and you can begin to look for information on each part.

The key words will indicate how you are to treat the subject (see above). The shorter the essay title, the more difficult it may be to decide on the scope of the essay. If you feel that the question is too broad and open-ended for you to know how to tackle it, ask the advice of your teacher or tutor.

Making a plan

First, write an outline of the basic structure of the essay. It often helps to talk this out with a fellow student. If you can explain your argument simply, you have a clear and logical essay plan, and only need to flesh it out with examples. Use a simple framework, such as:

A. Introduction
(i) Say exactly what you understand by the essay title, and what you think you are required to answer.
(ii) Say which aspects of the subject you are going to deal with, and why you have chosen these particular ones.

B. The main section of the essay
(i) Write down three or four main ideas which lead to a conclusion.
(ii) Support each idea with examples drawn from authors, statistics, case histories, personal observation or research.

C. Conclusion
(i) Give a summary of your main ideas.
(ii) Come to a firm conclusion if there is, in your opinion, an answer to the question. Many people recommend that you should write the last paragraph of your essay early on, so that you know exactly where you are heading and can keep firmly on track. You can always change the paragraph later, if necessary.

Writing the whole essay

Having read and selected material, made a plan and written your final paragraph, you can start writing the whole essay. Write it as well as you can, but regard it as a first draft and be prepared to change it later. Write simply and straightforwardly and be as concise as possible. Write as if you were writing for someone who knew nothing about the subject – don't leave the reader to fill in the gaps (s/he may not be able to!). Indicate the sources of any ideas you borrow from someone else. At the end of the essay list the books and articles you have been reading (this is called the bibliography). When you have finished the first draft of the essay, put it away for a few days, then look at it again. Read it out loud to see if the sentences 'flow' in a satisfactory way. Read it as if you were a stranger reading it for the first time, and ask yourself at the end what the essay was trying to say, and whether it said it clearly and convincingly. Did it answer the question set out in the title? Have you dealt with the subject in sufficient depth? If not, you've got a lot more work to do on it. Don't at this stage get impatient and rush the re-writing.

Making the final draft

Make sure your final draft is clearly written or typed. Check your spelling and punctuation. Tutors get impatient with work they cannot read easily and which is full of spelling or grammatical errors. If you are typing, take a carbon copy, then you needn't worry about the original getting lost (either by you or the tutor). If you don't type, take a photocopy of the essay. There are coin-operated photocopiers in most libraries now, and also in many colleges and individual departments.

Common errors in essay writing

- Some students give only generalizations, without adequate supporting arguments and examples.
- Other students give lots of facts, but no reasons. In other words, they forget the 'whys' and the 'hows'.
- Others write a number of almost unrelated paragraphs, which don't add up to a coherent statement about anything: they probably have not asked themselves the relevant questions about the essay title.

It's never too late ...

You probably won't believe this, but after you have polished and re-written your essay, your tutor will probably skim through it rapidly and pause only if you can win his or her attention with a really interesting idea. So you may as well chance your arm and make some provocative statement (providing you can back it up!). At least s/he will believe you have thought about the question.

Chapter 8
Getting the family on your side

The best help a mature woman student can get is the love and support of her family. Nowadays families come in all shapes and sizes. Marriage is still the most popular arrangement for the majority of men and women, and even when they break up most divorced people remarry. But many couples prefer to remain outside the bonds of marriage, and of course there are lots of single parents coping with children on their own. Some women live with other women, and some women live with their parents or other relatives. Whatever your situation, it is important to get your family on your side. Let them know what you want to do, and ask them to share your hopes and problems, then they can feel part of your great adventure in education.

In this chapter 'partner' will mean for most of you the man in your life, whether legal spouse or not, but could mean a relative or friend, too. 'Marriage' will mean any more or less permanent relationship between two people sharing home and possibly children.

Many women, of course, already have jobs, and have had to face up to the problems of combining home and outside work. If you are in that position and are already coping to your own satisfaction, you can skip this chapter. But even you will need to know that being a student is in some ways more demanding than a job outside the home. Students do not have fixed hours; they bring their work home with them; and frequently they work late to meet an essay or project deadline, or prepare for exams. When that happens, having the family on your side makes all the difference.

Does your partner understand you?

Have you ever discussed with your partner what you would like to do with your life, and how education could help you? Are you afraid to? Colleges report that many women who fail in their courses say they have never discussed their ambitions with their partners, who consequently never understood why they went to college in the first place. By contrast, women who succeeded said they had discussed their aims at great length with their partners, who had played an important supportive role by taking a large share of household and childcare responsibilities, or paying for outside help.

So it seems that a woman who becomes a mature student, and wishes to keep a good relationship with her partner has to decide early on to get him on her side. If he understands her needs and aims, and accepts them because he sees the strength of her commitment, he will probably be proud of her and keen to help. But this will require him to accept her as a person in her own right, with needs equal to his for emotional support – particularly at times when she feels vulnerable to criticism or competition, or even inadequate. The relationship between partners has also got to be flexible enough for them to accept changes in what have been their previously accepted and perhaps undisputed roles.

The ideal partner for a mature student is intelligent, sensitive, and naturally non-sexist. But it goes without saying that not every man is such a paragon of virtue, so you will probably have to overcome a certain amount of innate prejudice and fear of change in your man. Assuming that your partner is neither a saint nor a self-centred slob, how can you get him to understand your wish to 'break out' of a comfortable rut? What are you to do if his reactions are unexpectedly hostile?

First, you must try to understand what your partner is thinking and perhaps fearing. Marriage, or a similar close relationship, continues to be so popular (at least as an ideal) because most people need to share their lives with a sympathetic person who will also provide emotional support when needed. Not all men admit that this is a *reciprocal* need, however; many women make marriage their whole endeavour, providing the support for their menfolk who do not acknowledge how much they rely on the physical and mental support of their wives, and fail to understand that their wives also need support and understanding. Men usually have a separate world or work, and may not see how stifling domestic life alone can be.

Getting the family on your side

A man reared with the belief that a woman's place is in the home, putting first the interests of husband and children as an obligation not to be questioned, is going to have a lot of difficulty understanding and accepting a woman who wants to do something else with her life. He might wonder why she is looking for things to do on her own, instead of concentrating on the family. And he might think she intends to spend less time with them. Will she start to resent the domestic responsibilities when she compares her lot with that of unmarried students? He might think he is to blame, by not providing sufficient interest and attention, or he might worry that his friends and family will think there is something wrong with him as a husband and provider. He may even secretly worry that his wife plans to leave him eventually, and even if the relationship is bad he may not want to be the one who is abandoned. He may envy or resent his wife's opportunity to study, especially if he himself has not been to university or college. But even if he is a graduate himself, he may remember his own student days as ones of youthful fun and irresponsibility. Either way, he may not be sure how much housework and childcare will be expected of him. And if he and his wife are middle-aged, he may wonder why on earth she is taking up a whole new set of interests just when he is hoping to take it easy for a time. He might even be contemplating early retirement just when his wife is taking up an educational challenge.

Not all husbands have such negative feelings about their wives taking up new interests, however. Many see the possibility of their wives being happier, thereby benefiting the whole family. Some hope that their marriages will improve if there is more partnership between equals. And many hope that, when their wives earn a good salary, they will take over some of the family's financial burdens. More and more women are relieving their husbands of the responsibility of being the sole breadwinner. Men of quality, it is said, are not threatened by equality.

Of course, it is not easy to refute the strongly-held, often irrational gut reactions some men express about women, and arguments about women's capabilities do not always lead to harmony and good relations between men and women. So you must be as calm and reasonable as possible, but above all you must be *firm*, so that your husband takes your views seriously.

It's never too late ...

Then point out that being a student is going to help both of you, by making life more interesting. Here are some of the arguments you can use.

Becoming a student can benefit your marriage

Let's be clear about one thing: if your marriage is already on the rocks, becoming a student is not going to save it. Some women, it is true, have gone to college as an escape from an unhappy marriage, and have found, to no-one's surprise, that the change has only hastened the break. If two people are basically incompatible, nothing external to the relationship will hold it together. But if your marriage is sound at the core, even though it may have grown a little stale and lack some of its former zest, then becoming a student can only benefit both partners, in the new interest and understanding it can bring. Listen to some of the opinions expressed by mature women students who have already been through the experience.

"If the wife is happier, it is good for the husband too."
If you are feeling restless and frustrated in your life as full-time housekeeper, you are probably not the most pleasant person to have around. Once you have made up your mind to make a change and return to education, you will probably feel better about yourself and your contentment will spread to the rest of the family. Some women students find that they improve their relationship with partners as a result of unbottling their feelings and explaining their resentments. Many say that for years the husband realized that his wife was resentful, but they never talked about it. As students, however, women learn to express their feelings about all sorts of things, without getting 'all worked up', so they can argue more lucidly and objectively. They are also relieved to find that many other women have similar feelings; and husbands are less aggrieved when they find out that their own wives are not the only women who want more out of life than the housewife role.

"There's a lot more to talk about, apart from personal feelings,

when a wife is a student."

Many women report that their partners are really keen to hear all about what is happening in their college lives. Your partner may have been to college himself, and can indulge in a bout of nostalgia when you are talking about student concerns. Or he may fancy the idea of taking up a course of education himself, and be interested to see how the family takes to having a student parent. And he may get a lot of pleasure from sharing your new ideas, in which case you can make a point of discussing the course work in depth with him. He is probably used to hearing about your everyday chores, and finds that sort of conversation predictable and boring. But now you will have a whole new world of ideas to explore with him.

If, however, you have a partner who doesn't really want to talk about your college work, or finds your ideas threatening, you will have to go slowly, raising one subject at a time and getting his reactions. Ask his opinion on some of the ideas raised in discussions, beginning with the funny or outrageous ones. Let him see that they are new and unfamiliar to both of you, and that you are genuinely interested to hear what he thinks of them.

You will probably find that, as a student, you will have less time than before to spend with your husband, because essay writing and reading consume such a lot of your evenings. So it is up to you to make the time you *do* spend together more stimulating. But you must still make time to discuss *his* worries, and family matters, so perhaps you should come to an agreement to listen to each other in turn!

"You can learn to listen to each other, not talk to each other."
Think about this and be honest: are you so used to your husband's conversation that you feel you don't need to *listen* to him? Do you assume that you know what he is going to say, and mentally switch off? In fact, do you find you are not generally listening to what anyone else says, but perhaps working out what you will say when you next get the chance? Busy housewives and mothers, often trying to do too many things at once, are frequently so absorbed in their own problems that they listen with only half an ear to their families and friends. Women are not the only culprits in behaving in this way; indeed, the complaint of many women

It's never too late ...

is that their husbands do not listen to them. But we are all guilty of not listening intently to what others say.

As a student you will be encouraged and taught to express yourself verbally or in writing as clearly as possible: in other words, you will learn to communicate your thought to others. But you will not be taught to *listen* properly. You have to learn that for yourself. You may think this is not necessary, since most of us can stay silent whilst others talk. We don't interrupt; we wait our turn to speak; and we learn to look interested in what is being said, even if we have 'switched off'. But that is just a question of good manners. Real listening is an art. It is a lot more than polite silence. It involves trying to understand what people are really saying: what is behind their apparently flippant questions or remarks? And it involves not dismissing other people's opinions out of hand. You can put this skill to use in everyday life above all in your marriage.

In close relationships, in particular, there is a temptation to take it for granted that you are understanding and interpreting correctly what your partner is saying. Very often you may be getting it wrong, and it is a good habit, if you are not absolutely clear what the other person is trying to say, to go over the ground again. Say something like, "I think I know what you mean. Is it so-and-so?" Or ask outright, "do you mean such and such?" This may sound simple, but you will be surprised how often you are not getting the message correctly.

Learning to communicate in this way with your partner can be refreshing and stimulating to both of you. When you become a student, you may not have had the same education as your husband, or you may lack his confidence to express opinions. Or you may both lack formal education. You are going to need to clarify your thoughts constantly, in order to write them down. Always remember that if someone else does not understand you, it is *your* fault, not theirs. Words don't always mean what you *want* them to mean, and it is up to you to find a way to convey your meaning accurately. Ask your partner how something you have written sounds to him; tell him what you are trying to say, and then see if your written words convey that meaning. Explaining something to someone else is often the best way of getting a grasp on it yourself. And don't forget to tell your husband that, too!

Student mothers are better mothers

"My Mum's a student" is a great opening gambit at school, and children soon learn to be proud of their student mothers. Not everyone agrees, of course. Grandpa or mother-in-law may think you ought to be at home every minute, waiting for the children to come home. But in these days of working wives this is a very old-fashioned idea, and you should tell them so.

Most children seem more surprised than upset by their mother's decision to go to college. Many of them are frankly incredulous that anyone would *choose* to go back to school and take examinations. But underneath they may be worrying that you will have less time to spend with them – and indeed you will find it hard to do everything you want to do, or feel you ought to do, in the time available (but no more so than most working mothers).

Some mature women students worry so much about the possible harm they may be doing their children, that they completely forget the benefits that are being reaped. Take the trouble to explain to your children, if they are old enough, exactly why you want to be a student, and point out some of the benefits to all of you. If you believe in the value of education, for example, you couldn't set your children a better example than by going back to school yourself! Consider the following points, too.

You can be a better mother if you feel better about yourself
Children often come home from school exhausted, wanting only to unload their moans before dashing out to play with friends. The housebound mother may feel like a sponge, mopping up the children's irritations, and then being left to get rid of them as best she can. How much better for you all if you can both give sympathy and expect theirs in return – because you too know the problems of learning. This is what one teenage girl said about her feelings when her mother was a mature student:

"We all knew that Mum was working for something important to her, because she explained that education was something she really felt she needed. We saw how hard she had to work, and we all had to sacrifice quite a lot of family outings and so forth. Many times we couldn't get her attention, or Dad's either, because he was more busy too. But when Mum took her degree, and we all went along to see her get the certificate, we felt we had all contributed to her success. And we were very proud of Dad for the good job he had done looking after us while she studied."

You can be a good 'role model' for your children
If you believe that people should be more equal partners in marriage, and you want to change some of the entrenched views about what women should or should not do in life, this is your chance to do something about it. For example, along with other working mothers, you can help to dispel the notion of women as 'merely housewives'. It is good for children to see that marriage can be a partnership in which both men and women cook and clean, iron and look after children. You can show them that a mother does not exist simply to wait on them hand and foot. Show them that you are a human being with concerns of your own, and that you have rights as much as they do. Here is what two young children said they had learned from having a student mother:

"My Mum says that things have got to change in the home, not only for her sons but also for her daughters. When she became a student we all had to take a good share of the chores. The boys were upset at first, and I didn't think it fair because none of my friends have to help in the house. But we all got used to it, and realised how boring it is to do the same jobs week after week. I think the boys will have a different attitude towards their wives when they marry." (a 16-year old girl)

"I remember Mum telling us about a study of children in six countries, and how even 5 and 7 year olds were depended on to help care for younger children, to work on farms, to carry in wood, fetch water and prepare meals. Up to then we had grumbled if we were asked to make our beds! Anyway, it made us see that children in other parts of the world did a lot more than we did, and we agreed to help our parents by doing more in the house from then on." (a 15-year old boy)

You will feel close to your children when you are all learning
Many student mothers and children study together. Children are

Getting the family on your side

usually intrigued to see their mothers studying, and young children often imitate them by getting hold of books and settling down to read. If you are doing elementary courses or GCSE work, you may have a child doing similar work, and it can create a real fellow-feeling between mother and child if they can compare notes or study together. Your child can often help you over a hurdle because s/he has only recently experienced a similar learning difficulty, and you may find it easier to ask your child for an explanation than to ask your tutor – particularly if it is a relatively simple and basic step. And your children will greatly relish the chance to be your teacher from time to time! This mutual help can continue for a very long time if you go on to higher education when your child is becoming a student too. You can discuss different teaching methods and lecture styles, and compare notes on student life in general.

If your children are going through a phase of resenting school, you can encourage them a lot by your example to think of education as lifelong, pleasurable and desirable. Even if they decide to leave school at the earliest opportunity, they will have taken the point from you that it is possible to return to education later in life.

From your point of view as a parent, you will better understand some of the pressures on your children that result from school work and exams. You will identify with their bewilderment, confusion, concern about falling behind, exam nerves and so on. Suddenly, homework will be a reality for you, too. The generation gap will narrow dramatically when you have lessons, homework and exams in common with your children.

Your children will become more independent
Many women students say that their children become more self-reliant and take on more responsibility in the home. *Allowing* children to become more independent is one of he most difficult things for a mother to do, because it is hard to decide just when to begin, and at what stage you can delegate real responsibility. Success in doing this means that as a mother you have 'worked yourself out of a job', and many women feel this is a threat to their self-esteem and status as caring mothers. As a student mother, on the other hand, you will have so many things to do that you will

be delighted to offload some tasks on to the rest of the family, thus allowing your children to become more independent without your resenting it.

Most of us do far too much for our children when they are young. We do it with the best of intentions. We enjoy doing it, and they enjoy our attentions. But children have to start doing things for themselves some time, and we have to resist the urge to continue doing things for them because we can do them so much faster. This does not mean that we can or should expect too much of them too soon, but we should accept that we want them to be independent eventually, and let go the reins a bit at a time.

You will appreciate the time you spend with your children

We all know mothers who spend all day looking after their children, but no time playing with them. They often seem afraid that the playing will go on all day, so they refuse to get involved in painting, reading, singing nursery rhymes or constructing things. It is obviously difficult, too, for some mothers to enter into the world of the child, yet this is much more fascinating than housework, which goes on in the same relentless fashion long after the children have grown up and left home. If you don't find the company of small children at all stimulating now, it may be because they seem to dominate your whole life and attention. If you decide to go ahead and become a student, you will have less time available than previously to spend with your children, but you can make that time more pleasurable to both of you by devoting your whole attention to them. You *must* make the effort to give the children some of your time every day.

You can learn a great deal about your children by playing with them when they are young. When they are older, you can talk things over with them, but please listen carefully to what they are saying, without constantly interrupting or overriding their opinions. Ask them what they want to do in your time together: if they want help with homework, give it; if they want to play cards or scrabble, do it; if they want to play a pop record and get your opinion on it, listen to it. Whatever you are doing, give the children your undivided attention. Children can be stimulating and fun, as well as hard work. An hour of intense enjoyment is better than a whole evening of moaning, "What can we do?"

Getting the family on your side

Being human and normal, most children will hope that little is going to change in their lives as a result of your being a student, unless it is for the better. You are going to have to get the children on your side, as well as your husband, if the better things are to predominate. Tell them you need their positive support and love, but that in return you will do the same for them. They will be proud that you depend on them.

Chapter 9
Caring for the children

Becoming a student does not mean neglecting your children, any more than going out to work needs to do in this day and age of the working mother. No less than 19% of married women with dependent children now go out to work full-time and a further 39% work part-time in Britain, according to *Social Trends,* HMSO, 1992. They all have to make arrangements for having their children looked after (when the children are not in school), and if they can do it, so can you. The problems are more difficult if your child(ren) are under school age, but they are not insoluble.

Employment Training Scheme training courses (see Chapter 3) are all full-time, and this means from 9 a.m. to 5 p.m. or even 8 a.m. to 5 p.m. These courses are intended to be as much like work as they can make it. And they don't allow time off for school holidays. However, if you have a family to look after, a health problem or other special reason, you may be able to train part-time. If you do a training course when you have a pre-school child, you will need full day care. But some student mothers are well placed for looking after their children themselves for most of the week. For example, actual teaching hours on a full-time degree course are around 10 to 14 a week (up to 20 for laboratory sciences), admittedly sometimes awkwardly arranged, but not requiring you to spend all day, every day, at college. Your travelling time to and from classes will lengthen the periods you spend away from home, of course, and you may therefore need to study at a college as near to your home as possible, in order to cut travelling time. But student mothers can do a lot of their study at home, and of course academic terms at universities and colleges of education cover from 30 to 36 weeks of the year only. Vacations generally coincide with children's school holidays, though college don't usually have half-term breaks as schools do.

Some colleges have set up courses especially to suit mothers; the lectures are laid on between 10 a.m. and 3 p.m., so that you can see the children off to school in the mornings and be back home when they come in.

If you want to take courses which do not require you to find ways of having your children looked after, you can take a correspondence course (which tends to be very lonely) or Open University or Flexistudy courses (see Chapter 3) which combine learning at home with the chance to meet fellow students from time to time.

But assuming that what you really want is to get out of the house and meet people regularly, and to have time to savour a college life, you should think about the best ways to find good childcare facilities, and the benefits to both you and your children.

Care for the under fives

Of course, few mothers are immune from guilt feelings about what might happen when you have to leave very young children in the care of others. So they get very worried about whether and when they *can* go out to work or become a student. If you haven't got relatives or friends who will care for your child (and research by the Department of Employment shows that this is the most common form of childcare), you will be thinking about nursery care of various kinds. Quite apart from the need, there are many positive advantages for your children in a nursery environment.

Infant school teachers report that children who have been at home with their mothers constantly, may not have been encouraged to play with 'messy' things like paint and sand (because this makes extra cleaning work). Indeed, if they live in a flat or small house without a garden, they may be unused to playing at all, in the sense of having plenty of space in which to run about and play boisterous games. Many blocks of flats have signs on their green spaces saying, 'No ball games', which is terribly inhibiting.

Children living in homes large and small may not be used to shouting and singing as means of expression, if the parents do not like noise, or the neighbours complain. And in homes at all social levels, children are frequently kept quiet by being allowed to watch television for long periods (this may be very educative, but it is a passive rather than an active occupation). But at a nursery all kinds of play and exercise are possible, if it is well organized, and noise is expected.

Many parents are too busy with other things to tell stories to their children, to talk to them frequently, or to answer their endless questions. This may happen just as often where the mother is at home all day as where she works away from home, because not everyone *likes* dealing with small children or finds communication easy; and children from affluent homes are not necessarily any better off than children from poorer homes, in these respects. Infant teachers find that some children who come to school for the first time at age 5 have difficulty in communicating verbally with the staff and other children, and this is usually because the parents have not talked enough to the child. Some well-educated parents feel totally unable to enter into the world of a child, but they know that properly trained nursery staff will do that well.

However good and loving a mother you are, and however much time and attention you give to developing your children's skills and interests, you cannot teach them at home the social skills of getting on with other children (and adults) who are not members of the family. Your children need to play with other children – off their own home ground – and to share toys, activities and laughter. Children need to dress up and act parts, to hear music and talk to other children freely. And they need to learn to deal with conflict and hostility, too.

Don't expect nursery education to alter your child's mental ability, or assist the child to achieve greater academic success later in school, compared with the child who has been at home with mother up to the age of 5. But infant teachers are emphatic that children who have been in a nursery are generally more independent than others, and more self-assured in the early school days, being more confident with strangers and other children.

Even if your child does not greatly benefit from nursery school (in the sense of developing more skills), provided the child is not gravely unhappy there are unlikely to be any ill-effects. And that is what mothers mainly worry about.

The kinds of care available for under fives

Crèche: Crèche is French for manger or crib; a crèche accepts

It's never too late ...

babies and small children of working mothers (or others who need the facility) for the full day. It is not geared to make any educational provision. Similar to the crèche are the following:

Day nursery: Basically for pre-school children whose mothers are away at work. The children are well cared for, but the day nursery provides no education. Most day nurseries are run by local councils, but a number of factories provide day nurseries for their employees, and some colleges and universities have crèches and nurseries for staff and students. Fees are often geared to the parents' ability to pay.

Nursery: A term which can be applied to any place where young children are looked after.

Nursery classes: These are special classes attached to infant schools, making educational provision for children of pre-school age. They provide an early introduction to school, and of course no fees are charged. With 'falling rolls' (i.e. fewer children of school age) it is increasingly possible to get your child into school at around the age of 4.

Nursery schools: These are usually privately-run and charge fees. The word 'school' is misleading. There are no formal lessons, but children aged from two to five are supervised by trained staff and given a stimulating environment in which, through playing with paint, sand and water, for example, they can broaden their experience.

Playgroup: A group normally run by the parents, who charge a small fee for each child, and expect mothers or fathers to take turns assisting the supervisor who is in charge. They provide recreation and stimulus for children, usually taking only children aged over 3 years because of health regulations Playgroups may provide only one session a week, or as many as ten half-day sessions a week.

Childminder: A person who looks after a child or children not related, usually in his/her own home and for a fee. The childminder has an obligation to be registered with the local authority (though many are not) if they look after two or more children under five. The local authority then checks up on the safety aspects of the place where the children are being minded, for example, and this is a very valuable safeguard.

Baby-sitting: This term covers the sort of arrangement where you pay someone to come to your house to look after your child. You might choose to pay for childcare combined with some help with the housework. Clearly, what you are looking for here is a reliable person who you can trust and who likes taking care of children. You should regard the childcare aspect as more important than the enthusiasm for housework.

Nannies, nursery nurses: If you can afford to employ a nanny or nursery nurse, you can recruit through a specialized agency (there are lots of advertisements in *The Lady* weekly newspaper, obtainable form many newsagents), or through your local Jobcentre; or you can place an advertisement yourself in a newspaper; or you can approach one of the colleges which train nursery nurses (ask your local education authority for information); or you can ask your friends for the names of nannies they recommend.

A living-in nanny or nursery nurse will be very expensive, and you have to be sure that you have sufficient space in your home to accommodate her. (I have not so far heard of male nannies, though presumably men are not excluded from the job). It might be possible to get hold of a well-qualified nanny who continued to live in her own home, and worked for you only on weekdays; or you might find someone who was willing to stay with you all week, but wanted weekends away. The latter arrangements are more popular with young nannies than the full-time living-in arrangements; and from your point of view it would give you weekends free of sharing your home.

What are the realistic possibilities of childcare for under fives?

The local authority system
The system of *day-care* in Britain has far too few places to meet

It's never too late ...

the demand, according to a 1990 report by Peter Moss, Coordinator of the European Childcare Network. Only a third of mothers then wanting local authority day-care for their children had been able to find it.

All-day and all-year care for children under 3 in local authority day nurseries is available only to 'priority' categories of children. Places are not usually given to children from two parent families, just because both parents are working. 'Social need' defines the largest group of children accepted, and 'children of lone working mothers' is another category. You can always apply to your local authority, to find out their policy and the length of the waiting list.

If you have a child under 5, and would like a place in a *state nursery class or infant school*, you will find an extraordinary variation between local authorities, so you will have to check the practice in your area. Usually, 3 or 4-year olds attend school part-time (for about three hours a day), and the hours are rigidly fixed. You might find your child in school in the morning, whereas you had a class in the afternoon, so you would still need a childminder. But at least you could use the morning to get on with private study!

Community nurseries

In Inner London a number of 'community nurseries' have been established: these are experiments in cooperation between local authorities and groups of parents. They are housed in converted domestic housing, and relatively small groups of children (20 to 25) are involved. The nurseries are funded by local authorities, but parents and staff are involved in the management. Most do not take children under two – mainly because of lack of resources and specialized staff and accommodation required to meet the demanding care standards of young children. You could look around for one of these community nurseries if you live in Inner London.

Voluntary organizations

Some voluntary organizations provide childcare similar to local authority care, and for similar categories of children (such as Barnados, National Children's Homes and the Save the Children Fund), but their total pre-school provision is small.

The private sector
If you have no special claim on a council day nursery or a school place, or a place in a voluntary day-care centre (as above), you will have to turn to the private sector – or you may in any case prefer to do this. Here you will have a choice between:

Commercially-run nurseries which charge substantial fees; There were 2,165 private or voluntary nurseries registered to provide all-day care in 1990, permitted to care for 57,669 children. As with all childcare facilities, the quality of care is variable, though many offer a very good service.

College crèches or playgroups are provided by some colleges and universities. Ask the Student Union at the college which interests you if such a facility exists. Fees are fairly high but are often reduced if a student is in poor circumstances, and the Student Union at the college will help out with the fees in hardship cases.

Pre-school playgroups. Run by local groups of parents, the fees are generally low because playgroups like these are non-profit making, but you would have to take a turn at helping the supervisor look after the children.

Childminders, nannies etc. You can employ someone to look after your child, either in your own home or in the minder's home.

The Department of Health is responsible for the regulation and supervision of private nurseries, as well as the homes of those who, for a fee, look after more than two children under 5 years of age.

How to judge a good nursery environment from a bad one

Spend at least two hours at the centre, watching what happens
You need to spend a fairly lengthy time watching the way things go, before you have a good idea what the nursery is like. Notice how the staff deal with children who cry a lot, how they deal with temper tantrums or naughty behaviour such as fighting, spitting or throwing water and sand around. How do the staff behave when they are getting tired towards the end of a morning or afternoon session? You can learn a lot by watching how the staff behave towards each other, how the children interact, and how

the staff speak and act towards different children.

Do the staff really seem to like children? Do they encourage questions? Do they play with the children from time to time? Are they willing to comfort a child who is upset, by cuddling, hugging or holding hands for a time? Avoid a centre where you hear staff frequently telling children they are naughty or bad, especially if this is said in a very forceful manner.

Find out if the staff tend to stay for a long time, or if there are frequent staff changes.
It can be very upsetting for small children if there are constant changes in the staff, because just as they are getting used to one person they have to adjust to another.

Does the nursery welcome visits from parents, and their questions?
Whether your child spends a full day at a nursery, or only a few hours a week, you need to be able to speak to the staff about any questions that concern your particular child, and you need to be able to see how the nursery runs. I know you probably don't want to be labelled a troublemaker, thereby making things more difficult for your child, but it is very important for you to know that your child is happy and unafraid at the nursery.

Are the nursery premises safe?
Of course, the premises should be examined regularly by the Fire Officer, or a Safety Officer, but visits may occur only rarely and a lot can go wrong between visits. Have a look yourself at the precautions to guard power points. What is the form of heating, and are there any hazards? Is the play equipment in good shape and free from sharp or jagged edges?

If the nursery is owned by the council, you can make any complaints you may have direct to the council office, or to a councillor. If the nursery is privately owned, or part of a village hall, for example, you should report your worries to the local Safety Officer or Fire Officer.

Does the nursery encourage children to explore different activities?
Beware of a nursery where the TV is on for a long time, or where children are expected to sit quietly or rest on beds for long periods.

Are there both indoor and outdoor play areas at the nursery?
Children need to spend some time running around out of doors, playing in a sand pit, playing on a swing, or just playing 'tag'. Even a short break allows them to air their frustrations. And from the point of view of the staff it reduces the noise level in the indoor area for a period, and gives time to ventilate the room.

Can a child get away from the crowd?
Some nurseries have a small space as a quiet area, where a child can go to be alone. It might be a separate room, or just a hideaway box, a pile of pillows to form a nest, or a big cardboard box to sit in. It can even be a 'clothes maid' draped with a piece of material, which cuts off a little space and behind which the child can hide and not see anyone, or be seen.

You may have to look carefully at several nurseries before deciding which one will suit your own child. Don't feel you are being too fussy: it is important to find a good nursery because if your child is unhappy you will feel guilty and unhappy yourself. If you haven't used a nursery or playgroup before, try to get your child fixed up happily well before you start your student days, otherwise you might find yourself wasting a lot of valuable time on this particular crisis.

What makes a good childminder?

Because of the shortage of places for children in nurseries and day-care centres, parents turn to childminders. Over 200,000 children were placed with registered minders in 1990. Standards of care vary. Many childminders are women who, lacking other employment opportunities and with children of their own, find childminding an acceptable form of employment which fits in with their domestic circumstances. A National Childminding Association has been formed, to press for improved conditions, pay and status for its members. A number of local authorities are experimenting with support schemes for childminders: the authority trains the minders and this includes sending them to a local day nursery, to improve the quality of their care. More schemes like this would do much to remove the concern about childminders which many people feel. As I mentioned earlier, childminders are supposed to be registered with the local authority, but it is estimated that unregistered childminders much outnumber registered ones. In any case, registration does not amount to a guarantee of quality. An average charge for childminding in 1992 was £55 a week, but there was considerable variation around the country.

A good childminder is someone you can trust to treat your child well. Look round her house to see if there are plenty of toys and a safe playing area. Are open fires guarded? Is she patient and attentive to the children? However desperate you are, don't settle for someone you think unsuitable.

How can you help your small child adjust to being looked after by someone else?

1. Say goodbye when you leave your child: don't sneak off in an attempt to keep the child from crying. Children whose parents leave without telling them are never sure *when* they are going to be left, and they become anxious and clinging all the time.

2. Remind your child that you will be coming back later. Say a specific time, if you can. Some children really fear that parents won't come back to get them, and the fear is particularly strong if the child has been naughty.

3. Provide your child with some link to home (a favourite toy, a blanket, something of yours).

4. If possible, get one of the nursery staff to feel specially responsible for your child – someone to turn to if s/he feels tired or sad, and who will tell you if your child has had a quarrel or a fight.

5. Be patient about your child's way of greeting you and saying goodbye. Children often develop rituals to help themselves over the strain of leaving home and entering the nursery: these might include running and hiding, or hugging parents over and over again.

6. Never talk of leaving your child at the nursery as a sort of

punishment, or s/he will never settle down happily.

7. Watch for the signs that your child is seriously unhappy about going to the nursery. Here are some signals:

does s/he refuse to get up or get dressed in the morning?

does s/he seem unusually quiet or unhappy?

does s/he cry more easily, refuse to be comforted, cling to you for no apparent reason?

does s/he frequently protest when left at the nursery (crying, clinging, having tantrums)?

has s/he reverted to babyish behaviour such as thumb or finger sucking (assuming s/he is past that stage), or wetting pants?

has s/he become less active, less interested in things (wants to spend more time in bed, and play less)?

has s/he begun to do self-damaging things like head-banging, or having a lot of accidents?

8. If you notice any of these signals, and are sure that your child is not ill and needs a doctor, try one of the following remedies:

- Plan to spend 10–15 minutes each morning talking to and playing with your child before you leave home. Talk of the things you will do together later in the day.
- Plan to spend the first 15 minutes at the nursery *with* your child: a brief adjustment period with you nearby may make your child feel much more secure.
- Try to cut down on the number of hours your child needs to spend at the nursery. A full day of separation is difficult for a child under 3 years old.
- Consider enrolling your child in a different nursery. Studies of various nurseries have found that only a minority provide really excellent care, but there are many good ones around. The quality is not always related to the fees charged, either: some of the best charge least and some of the worst charge most. So choose carefully. A good yardstick is that the quality of the staff counts for more than the visible facilities, though

the latter are important too.

Conclusion: Becoming a student when your children are under school age is perfectly possible provided you can either: (a) afford to pay for childcare; (b) qualify for a place in a council nursery; (c) have a partner, friend or relative who will look after the children; (d) can arrange to do reciprocal childcare for someone who also wants to be a student. On most courses you will not need to be away from home all day and every day, anyway. The exceptions are the training courses under the Employment Training Scheme, which are as full-time as a job would be. But if you want to be a student and need childcare, the possibilities certainly exist for you.

Care for the over fives

Most women reckon it is easier to become a student when their children are all at school. But you still need to think of the times when the children are ill, and of what they will do after school on days when you have late classes. Colleges do not usually have half-term holidays as schools do. These will not be all-year-round problems for you as a student, but where would you get help if you needed it? A good arrangement is to have a friend who will stand in for you at odd times (perhaps with your doing the same in return) whom, say, the school can telephone if your child should be sick. If not, there *are* other possibilities:

Local authority play centres
These are intended for (paid) working mothers, and operate after school and during school holidays. They are the most widespread of the various provisions. The centres often occupy a room or hall in a school, plus the playground. The staff are paid, and there are usually between 50 and 100 children attending the centre. Even in the areas of the most dense provision not every school has a centre. No provision is made for getting children to the centres, but they do not charge fees and are open to all children.

Provision is patchy, and the government has only a vague idea of which LEAs provide such services and to what standard, but

Caring for the children

London and Liverpool have provided such services since before the First World War. Most centres are in urban areas.

Voluntary play centres
There is a wide range of holiday playschemes run by voluntary bodies and charities such as Dr. Barnado's and the Church of England Children's Society. The schemes are often grant-aided by local authorities and/or the Urban Aid programmes. They are variable in type, but usually operate for school hours during holidays, with a handful operating after school in term time.

Adventure playgrounds
There are supposed to be just under 300 adventure playgrounds in operation, of which about 90 are in London. Since they operate on a come-as-you-please basis and cannot guarantee parents the security of knowing where your children are at a particular time, you would have to arrange for a friend or child of responsible age to accompany them.

Children's houses
These schemes are attempts to run comprehensive, out-of-school care services, covering after-school hours and right through the holidays, in a house rather than an institutional setting. The Gingerbread Corner at Croydon, for example, picks up children after school in a minibus, guarantees the whereabouts of the children, uses paid staff and runs throughout the year. Because it is a completely self-help project, Gingerbread Corner has to make a charge for attendance.

Tagging on
This is a scheme whereby older brothers and sisters, of children under 5 who have day-care centre places, are allowed into the centre after school. This is fairly common in day-care centre run by charities, particularly the National Childrens' Homes.

What if there are no organized after-school activities in your area?
1. You could pressure your local authority to use school buildings more extensively for this purpose. According to the Fair Play for Children Campaign, a majority of shire counties and metropolitan

It's never too late ...

districts "approve in principle" the dual use of school buildings as schools and play centres, so check up on the attitude of your local council.

2. Unless and until council facilities exist, you are going to have to help yourself or enlist others to help you. The choices for you as a student mother are to:

- Skip late classes at the college, or try to get the times of late seminars changed. Ask the lecturer to tape-record any lectures you have to miss, and to make the tape available through the departmental office. Some departments already do this, not only for mature students who have to rush home for children, but also for any students who have a timetable clash.
- Arrange with a friend in similar circumstances to do reciprocal child-minding with you.
- If one child is old enough to take care of the others (which legally means over 13) let them come home from school, eat a snack, then watch TV or get on with homework. You could tell them to stick to cold drinks, and make sure there is sliced bread available, so you don't have to worry about them boiling a kettle or using a carving knife.
- Pay the teenage child of a neighbour to cover the after-school period for you.

In addition, you should talk to the children's teachers and head teachers, explaining that you are a student. Tell them when you will be away from home, and provide them with the telephone number of someone whom they can contact in an emergency (your husband, or a friend, or someone at your college who would give you a message).

A telephone in your home is invaluable if you want to keep in touch with the children when you have to stay over at college, and in case of any emergency within the home (for the use of the children themselves, or a childminder, to call for help). For your own peace of mind, hang a large notice by the telephone, giving useful phone numbers which can be called in an emergency and advising how to go about calling for help. For example, the following might be the kind of information to put up:

Caring for the children

When Mum and Dad are not at home ...
   NEVER LET STRANGERS INTO THE HOUSE

Important Telephone Numbers

Mum	....	Grandparents	....
Dad	....		....
Neighbours	....	Schools	....
	....		....
	....	Taxi	....

Dial 999 for Fire
Police Ambulance

Doctor ....

How to make an emergency call:

1. Take your time, stay as calm as possible and dial the number carefully to avoid making a mistake.
2. Explain the kind of emergency, not the kind of help you need. For example, say "a child has swallowed poison", not, "send a doctor".
3. Don't hang up until told to – you want to be sure the person you're talking to gets all the necessary information. Be sure to give your name, address, and telephone number.
4. If possible, send someone outside to direct the help you have asked for.

Conclusion: You should not have too many problems in making arrangements for your school-age children in their out of school hours. But if you are really worried and can't get anyone else to look after them, you should skip late classes at college and ask for lectures to be tape-recorded so that you can listen to them another time.

If you haven't got one already, try to get a telephone installed, so that you can keep in touch with the children. Take great care about making the house as safe as possible against accidents (no open fires, and teach them not to boil kettles or use carving knives when they are young). And above all, teach your children not to

It's never too late ...

allow strangers into the house, whatever story they are told. Instruct them to check up by telephone before admitting any official.

For further information you could contact the National Childcare Campaign, established in 1980 to work for childcare affordable by all parents, or its sister organisation the Daycare Trust, founded in 1986. The address for both is Wesley House, 4 Wild Court, London WC2B 5AU.

Chapter 10
Sharing the housework

Most students these days have to do some domestic chores. Even Royal Princes make their own beds when they are undergraduates, as do all students living in halls of residence. Accommodation for those living on campus is usually of a self-catering variety. And the majority of students who live in and around their colleges rent flats or houses with other students and do their own cooking, washing and cleaning. More students than you might think share a flat with someone of the opposite sex. Few young students want to spend much time on housework, no doubt feeling they have more interesting and important things to do, though many seem to enjoy cooking.

Mature women students are, or can be, different from younger students in two ways. First, they may have children as well as a partner. Secondly, they mostly live at home and may have long distances to travel to classes. That means they have to be *more organized* than most students, who often just let things slide. And, like students who share accommodation, they must insist on fair shares all round of the domestic chores.

Of course, this may be more difficult for a married woman of the traditional kind – and the older you are the more traditional you, and still more your husband, are likely to be. If you have been working at a paid job outside the home you have probably got things organized already – though magazine surveys show that women still appear to do more than their share of the domestic chores. If you have *not* been working outside the home for some time – say, since the children were born – then you have probably got into the habit of doing most of the basic chores and of being grateful – too grateful, perhaps? – for a bit of help with the dishes or the garden. Either way, becoming a student must be treated as a job – a real full-time job if you are a full-time student – and it requires at least as much organizing of the housework as any other full-time job outside the home.

Here again, it is important to get the family on your side, and convince them that if they share the eating, the clothes-wearing, and the house-messing, they must share the cooking, the washing and the cleaning too. Don't try to be a Superwoman and do it all yourself. No-one is going to give you a medal if the house "shines like a new pin" or if "you can eat off the kitchen floor". Houses are *not* mirrors for Narcissuses, and even the most houseproud people *don't* eat off the kitchen floor, whatever they say. Most husbands and practically all children secretly dislike wives and mothers who are *too* houseproud, because they are so uncomfortable to live with. In any case, the family will appreciate you all the more when they share the chores and know what an effort it takes to clear up after themselves.

When all is said and done, there are only two alternatives:

you can "let the house go to pieces" and learn to live in a messy home; or
you can plan and organize, and get the family to organize with you.

If you choose the first, you will no doubt have more than your share of complaints, crises and quarrels, but you will need no advice from outsiders – except, perhaps, the name of a good psychiatrist! But if you choose the second, there are a lot of tips you can learn from someone who has been through it all, and these are what this chapter is about.

Organize

Organization is a skill, like riding a bicycle. It takes a little training and intelligence, but the great majority of people can manage it if they try. Expect a few spills at first, but you'll soon get the hang of it and then you'll be up and away at speed. Don't worry if some people think it's unfeminine to plan and organize (in fact, women have always been better organizers than men, but that's *our* secret). In great-grandmother's day it was thought unfeminine for women to ride bicycles, and still more to do it more efficiently by wearing 'bifurcated nether garments'; but people soon got used to it and women cyclists became the symbol of 'the New Woman'.

Sharing the housework

When it comes to planning household chores, there is no 'one best way' and each family can look for a life-style which suits it, and keeps friction at a minimum. When you and your family are thinking of ways to reorganize your lives so that you have time for study, remember that too much organization is as bad as too little; you want to control your lives without becoming compulsive clock-watchers, and you don't want to be so tied to routine that you can't cope with a change of plans. But organization is necessary, and the first thing to do is to decide how much time you need for study. This will depend on the courses you take. As a guide, remember:

- Full-time students should aim to spend 35 to 45 hours a week on academic work, including lectures, seminars, laboratory work and private study.
- Part-time and home study students will probably need to spend 10 to 20 hours a week on academic work.

So when you have made up your mind which courses you want to take, you can work out how many hours in the week you need to devote to study, and you can divide that amount into daily stints.

Finding time for study

Find out where you are wasting time

If you think you can't find time to study during the day, you'd better have a good long look at how you are spending your time at present. How much time do you spend on household tasks? Very few women have any idea about this, so in other words they literally "don't know where the time goes". Management experts in industry urge their clients to keep a close watch on the time they devote to each task, and indeed recommend that they keep detailed time records. In that way they can see exactly where their time is going. Why don't you do something similar? Keep a detailed record of how you spend your time in a complete, fairly normal week. It will probably be an eye-opener to you. You can either destroy the record, if it is too shamefully full of hours you

It's never too late ...

can't really account for, or you can show it to your family as evidence of how long the domestic chores take (or how long you spend listening to the family's concerns). If the record is to be at all useful, it has to be made up of really detailed notes, such as:

Activity	Time you finish it	Length of time spent
Sleep	7.30 a.m.	8 hours
Washing & dressing	8.00 a.m.	½ hour
Breakfast	8.30 a.m.	½ hour
Read paper	9.00 a.m.	½ hour
Wash dishes	9.30 a.m.	½ hour
Tidying up	10.30 a.m	1 hour
Daily shopping	11.15 a.m.	¾ hour
Coffee with friend	12 noon	¾ hour
Collect child from school or playgroup. Prepare and serve lunch.	1.30 p.m.	1½ hours

You may be shocked to find how much time you spend on certain chores such as washing, ironing, cleaning windows, food preparation, washing dishes. If you want to make time to study, it will be a good thing to decide which of these jobs is really *necessary*, which could be done less regularly, and which could be delegated to others.

Make up a new weekly timetable for yourself and try it out

1. List activities which you can't easily change, such as the time for you and other family members to get up and leave the house. Put down mealtimes to which you are all accustomed, the times when children have to be taken to school or playgroup (and collected), times for taking relatives to a day care centre or for regular hospital appointments, for example.

2. Put down the time of colleges lectures or seminars, allowing adequate time to travel to college and back, if you are taking a course outside the home. Otherwise put down times of appropriate Open University radio or TV broadcasts, if these are the courses you have chosen.

Sharing the housework

3. Divide the remainder of your time between private study, social life, and household duties.

Make a virtue out of doing alternate academic and domestic work. Many writers and creative artists say they like to do manual work, such as gardening or woodwork, to relieve the strain of constant mental activity. You, too, could learn to turn from problem-solving or essay-writing to household chores – and without necessarily turning off your thought processes completely. Let you academic work and housework dovetail, and you will find that they harmonize better than you might expect.

Make a realistic timetable that you can stick to (unless you are ill). Don't budget every minute of every day to useful purposes, because it just won't work. Keep in mind which are the most important tasks you need to do in a particular day, and keep flexible periods for use as you please. If you allow for distractions such as phone calls, dealing with odd visitors or chatting with a friend, you won't find yourself falling behind schedule all the time.

Note the following points carefully when you are planning your week.

Private study
- Give private study priority over other home activities, wherever possible.
- Try not to do more than 8 hours' academic work in any one day. On the other hand, make sure you allocate usable periods for study of about 1 to 2 hours at a time. Periods of less than an hour are not much use except for sorting out notes, checking a booklist, reading the odd review, etc.
- Don't study for more than 3 hours without then taking a break.
- Dole out your private study hours to give roughly the same amount of time to each course you are taking; don't skimp on the time you spend on courses you don't like as much as others.
- Bear in mind that study hours are best if they come early in the day, when your concentration and attention are at their peak. So don't start your day with a heavy spell of housework. These chores can be done later in the day when your brain

It's never too late ...

is too tired to study further and your body needs a change. Tell yourself that the sooner the housework is done, the sooner the dirt will accumulate again, so why rush at it?

- If you are an early riser, could you get up long before the rest of the family and do 1½ to 2 hours' study then? Set your alarm for 6 a.m. and start reading as soon as you have made a cup of tea or coffee. Don't say you can't do this until you have tried to make it a regular part of your life. You could break from your studies to eat breakfast with the family, then return to study or go off to college.
- If, like me, you are not an early riser and can't turn yourself into one, could you work for an extra couple of hours most evenings when the rest of the family is in bed? Try to do an extra stint from, say, 11 p.m. to 1 a.m. If this makes for a disturbed night's sleep, however, scrap the idea.
- Allow time for relaxation between bouts of study. If you hate wasting time, remember that time spent in rest and quiet is not wasted, because you get real benefit from it and study better afterwards.

Social life

Social life means time to spend with your husband and children as well as meeting friends and relations or going to the theatre or cinema. Make sure you allocate special time to spend with your immediate family, because you will both enjoy it and they will resent it if you seem to push them aside completely in order to get on with your studies. And be prepared for times when children need extra time and attention, maybe because they feel hurt and neglected. You may find it best to devote the whole weekend to your family, if that is their only free time to be with you.

Social life also mans time you might spend at college, having coffee or a drink with fellow students, or joining in college activities, though many of these fall naturally between classes. You will have read about this in Chapter 6.

Household duties

There are a number of strategies for relieving yourself of some of the household chores, and most of them involve getting other people to help:

The family. Decide which are the hard-core jobs which have to be done around the house and garden, and then bring the family together to agree who will:

make the beds each day
change the bedclothes each week or fortnight
do the daily washing-up
cook the meals
wash the clothes
do the ironing
do the mending
do the major shopping
make up fires or stoke the boiler
feed the pets/exercise the dog
mow the lawns or weed the garden
clean the house
clean the car.

If your children are very young, you have to decide:

who will take them to nursery or infant school and collect them
who will bath them, or see that they have a wash and clean their teeth before going to bed
who will read their bedtime story
who will listen to them read aloud
who will take them for walks, or to visit friends etc.

When you have decided who will do which job, you can write it down on a calendar or make a wheel-within-a-wheel that turns to the names of different members of the family if you want to rotate the jobs between them each week or month. Try to give each member of the family a job that is not too unpleasant for that individual. But if everyone opts for clean and easy jobs, leaving you all the dirty ones, you'll have to put your foot down and insist on sharing all the jobs.

Even small children can help around the house, if you make it a game instead of a battleground. You can insist that they don't throw their dirty clothes down on the bedroom floor and expect someone else to pick them up; that they wash their own dishes after snacks; and that they don't abandon board games in the middle of the dining table. Both boys and girls can learn to sew on buttons, cook simple dishes, do the ironing. Be generous in your praise and tactful in your criticisms of their efforts, but don't let them get away with slipshod work which increases your workload.

As far as cleaning the house is concerned, you could perhaps decide in future to have a Saturday morning 'blitz' on it, but not bother too much during the week. That way, cleaning won't seem endless. Go out to lunch afterwards, perhaps, or buy fish and chips, as a good way to end the cleaning routine.

Your house may not look as good as you would ideally like it to, but if you can run it as a cooperative venture you will shed that feeling of being constantly on house duty.

If appeals to their good nature or sense of fair play do not work in getting your children to help with the chores, why not offer them small financial or other inducements for doing them? *You* probably don't enjoy doing the jobs, so why should they? Some parents, I know, disapprove of paying children for their help, but what's wrong with getting a willing helper instead of a resentful one?

Paying someone else. If there is enough money in the family budget, you can consider paying someone else to do some of the household work. Don't worry too much about the ethics of paying someone else to clean your house or do the gardening. After all, you wouldn't hesitate to pay a plumber or decorator, if necessary, so why think it wrong to pay a cleaner? Provided you are paying a fair rate for the job, you will find people willing to work for you.

If you have a room in your house which you could let, consider offering it free to a hard-up student who would welcome living there in return for help with the housework, childcare, and/or gardening.

Team work. One possibility is for a group of friends to meet in one of their houses and give it a thorough cleaning, then repeat the process at another house the following week, and so on round the group. For some people this is more interesting than cleaning by themselves, particularly if there are small children in the households who can play together under the supervision of one adult.

An alternative is for you to team up with a friend, or group of friends, and divide up household chores so that each person does what s/he dislikes least in each home. It is a form of specialization which works well for some people; it seems that some people enjoy ironing and will take over that chore for several households, if someone else will do the garden or clean the windows. Others will cook in return for having some mending done. I would find it hard to believe that team work such as this would work, had I not seen it operating successfully among groups of mature students.

Time-saving tips: shopping

1. Plan a whole week's menus. Do a large shop one day for all dry and tinned goods. Plan a smaller shopping trip for fresh meat and vegetables. Anyone with a fridge can keep fresh food for 3 to 4 days. A small freezer would be useful for storing bread and convenience foods for when you don't feel like cooking.

2. If you share your home with someone else, try shopping for each other in turn, leaving the other free for other chores. Or, you can take someone along with you to help, which will save time and energy (particularly if the other person is the car driver!).

3. Make sure that you keep in extra supplies of food, and at least one extra meal (tinned or frozen) so that you don't have to dash off to the shops at the last moment if you come home late.

4. Keep a list of household requirements on a wipe-clean noticeboard in the kitchen (you could, for example, use a child's 'magic marker' board). Tell whoever is responsible for the major shopping expedition of the week to transfer this information to a shopping list, just before going out, and to wipe the board clean at that stage.

5. Find a shop which will deliver an order for you, for emergencies when everyone is very busy or the car has broken down, say.

Time-saving tips: cooking

1. If you like cooking, spend time on it. But if it is a drag, buy

It's never too late ...

ready-prepared food when you entertain or want a treat. Find a shop which makes its own cakes and bread, and buy its products as special treats, even if they are too expensive for everyday use.

2. If you and your family really pine for the taste of home cooking, buy home-made jams, marmalade, pickles, cakes etc. at local sales of work, bring-and-buy sales, and other fund-raising events. Schools, churches, scout troops, as well as dozens of charities, constantly put on these events and advertise them in local newspapers. If you don't want to go to them, your children would probably love to go foraging for you.

3. If you have a freezer, you can do a large batch of baking from time to time, perhaps getting the whole family to take part in a bake-in. Vacations are a good time for a mature student to get the freezer stocked up.

4. Boil huge batches of potatoes at a time. Some of the left-overs can be sliced and fried. Some will make potato salad. Some will go into bubble-and-squeak. Children usually enjoy this kind of fry-up meal, because it is quickly prepared and they can do it for themselves.

5. Invest in an electric slow-cooking pot, powered by the equivalent of a light bulb, which can be left on all day without worry and which will mean there is a hot meal ready when you all arrive back in the evening.

6. Invest in a pressure cooker if your family want to cook meat and vegetables but tend only to think of it just before the meal is due to be eaten.

Time-saving tips: housework

1. Wrap up and put away any ornaments, silver, brass etc. which needs constant cleaning. Then you won't constantly worry about not getting round to doing these chores.

2. Try and buy bedlinen, shirts, blouses, dresses etc. made of no-

iron materials. This will save you hours of work.

3. Buy socks reinforced with nylon that don't go into holes right away.

4. Buy a dishwasher if all the family hates washing-up and getting the job done is a nightly battle. This is fairly expensive and only feasible if you have plenty of crockery and cutlery, but you may prefer this kind of help to help with the housework.

5. Make use of the service wash facility at the launderette; it costs little more to leave your laundry and collect it later, than to stay and look after it yourself. If you have a washing machine but no drying facilities, send the children to the launderette with your wet laundry, and let them use the dryers there. Better still, buy a tumble dryer if you can afford it (in the British climate it seems an essential) and don't have festoons of wet clothing round the house.

You can use the inexpensive coin-operated dry cleaning machine at the launderette for batches of sweaters, blankets etc., instead of washing them at home.

Chapter 11
Looking ahead – applying for jobs

By the time you finish your education, you may know exactly what you want to do. In fact, you may:

— be returning to a job and applying for promotion;
— have acquired definite qualifications making you eligible for a specific job (say, a GCSE in book-keeping, or a law degree);

But most women want a job, but don't exactly know what. And for them there is a lot of advice available. Don't forget, either, that by the end of your course you may be so in love with being a student that you want to stay that way for life!

Sources of careers advice

College Careers Service
(a) Initial interview to try and guide you into particular areas.
(b) If you are a graduate you can use Gradscope, a computerized system for which you pay a small fee, fill in a lengthy form, and later get a list of suggested occupations compiled by a computer.
(c) The college will probably have loads of leaflets available, with the widest possible details of job requirements and specifications, and a library of careers advice books and directories.
(d) The colleges arrange for employers or their representatives to visit the college and talk to students about possible job openings.

The Local Authority Careers Service
The Careers Service says it will give advice to adults as well as that for school leavers; their vocational guidance and practice in interviewing techniques are equally useful to the young and older job seekers.

It's never too late ...

Careers officers are compiling information on the attitudes of employers to mature entrants, on any age limits for jobs that they impose, and how they regard married women as employees. Research has shown that some employers actually prefer to employ older women.

Careers libraries have purchased books specifically geared to mature changers.

The National Advisory Centre on Careers for Women
This centre publishes a booklet entitled *Returners*, which describes career possibilities and the training needed for them.

Their advice service, for which you would need an appointment, covers educational choices, career changes, retraining and part-time work.

Write to them at 251 Brompton Road, London SW3 2HB, or telephone (071) 589 9237.

Private agencies
There are two kinds of fee-paying private agencies. One type offers full counselling and guidance, and you would expect them to organize workshops on topics such as career development, how to present your qualifications and job experience, and interviewing techniques. You would pay the agency a fee for their services.

The other type is known as a placement agency; they try to fit you to a job which is 'on their books', and the fees are paid by the potential employers.

Note If you meet any difficulty in getting careers advisers to treat you sympathetically, as an older woman wanting to find a job, go somewhere else right away. Don't however, assume that men counsellors will be unsympathetic: many of them have wives and mothers who work, after all. You may have to look around a bit to get really positive help, but it will be worth the effort.

Hunting for jobs

Jobcentres
Most people looking for a job would go to the local Jobcentre, run by the Department of Employment. They will tell you about job

vacancies, and may have available just what you are looking for. If not, one of their Restart courses, lasting four or five days, could help you decide what you are good at and what action to take in your search for a job. Job Search Seminars offer two days of expert help on the best ways to search out and apply for jobs, and what to do at job interviews. Job clubs show you how to perform well on the telephone and at interviews, and how to write a more effective job application. For job hunting you can use the Jobcentre's stationery, stamps, telephones, newspapers and other resources, free of charge.

The Training and Enterprise Councils (TECs) in England and Wales, and local enterprise companies in Scotland, directed by business and community leaders, aim to help you develop your skills. If you have special needs or difficulties in getting work because of a health problem or disability, the local Disablement Resettlement Officer (DRO) can advise you and help you find a job. The Sheltered Placement Scheme enables people with severe disabilities to work in a variety of jobs alongside the rest of the workforce.

The press
Watch the newspapers and specific journals every day for job advertisements, and apply right away unless the closing date for applications is way ahead. Job hunting can become a full-time occupation if you want to explore all the avenues and choices of jobs.

Graduate recruitment programmes
As the name implies, this is a service for graduates only, and information about available jobs is given to universities and colleges of higher education.

Writing direct to employers
What you are trying to do is make a job for yourself. You want to persuade an employer that you have special skills that make it worth creating a job for you.

Personal contacts
It goes without saying that you should use personal contacts to find out what jobs are available, or any openings that might be

coming up. You will find many people anxious to help you if they can, and most people respond to an appeal for help.

Note While you are looking for work, you can do voluntary work directly or indirectly related to the kind of job you want to do, as valuable experience that you can talk about in job interviews. Many voluntary organizations do pioneering work which the state services do not provide, and there are hundreds of 'good causes' which just cannot go on without voluntary help. Think how much the community gets by way of voluntary service from parish, district or county councillors, school governors, magistrates, teachers of English to immigrants, and those who work for the citizen's advice bureaux and the marriage guidance council, for example.

Job applications

The object of job applications is to get an interview. So you need to interest a potential employer enough to offer an interview. Make sure the notepaper you use is of good quality, and that your handwriting or typing, your spelling and punctuation, are impeccable. Be interesting, informative and enthusiastic – and be as concise as possible. Read out your letter of application aloud, and ask yourself if *you* would find it interesting.

Covering letter

When you first enquire about a job vacancy, you may be sent a form to fill in, or you may simply be asked to forward relevant details. Either way, write a covering letter – bright and brief – drawing attention to certain details of your experience that are relevant to the job you are applying for. Emphasize your strengths rather than your weaknesses. For example, if you have had a lot of job changes, make clear that you are seeking wide experience. Don't let it seem that you soon got bored with jobs.

The tone of your letter should be geared to the type of organization you are writing to: if it is a bureaucracy, don't make jokes; if you are writing, say, to an advertising agency you can take more risks.

Looking ahead – applying for jobs

Application form
How you fill it in depends on the form but type it if you possibly can. Answer all the questions, and if you think there is insufficient room to put something relevant, attach a separate piece of paper.

Curriculum Vitae (CV)
This Latin term is commonplace, meaning 'the course of life' so don't be afraid of it. It is a way to give concise information about what you have done in life If you prepare a number of copies, you can reply quickly to advertisements, by writing an individual covering letter tailored to the particular job. Make really good photocopies not carbon copies.

A good tip is to get someone who knows you really well and likes you to look over your draft CV. Everyone plays down experiences, and you want to be seen in the best light possible, so get someone else to paint you in the most glowing terms they can think of.

Your CV should contain:

Name
Address and telephone number
Date of birth ⎫ You could leave this out if you wish.
Marital status ⎭ Age may be an important concern for some jobs but marital status is not.
Nationality
Education (put early and late periods)
Work experience (paid and voluntary). Account for all periods of your life, and see that dates 'fit'. Add your experience looking after home and children as positive experiences.
Skills and other qualifications, such as music, typing, foreign languages, DIY skills.
Activities and interests. Basically, anything relevant, which doesn't fit in other categories, e.g. P.T.A. Committee, Sports.

Tip: don't list too many hobbies such as stamp collecting; it will look as if all your time is already occupied. You can't have too many *activities*, but you can have too many hobbies.

It's never too late ...

Points to watch

- Type your CV rather than write it. (You might be able to use the typewriter in the college office.)
- Use lots of white space. Don't cram the page. Imagine it is a page of a magazine and make it look appealing.
- Use capitals for sub-headings, and lower case for the actual information.
- Get the best possible photocopies, so they look like top copies.

Interviews

1. Never forget that an employer is weighing you up during an interview. But you are also weighing up the organization. You don't have to work for someone you hate.

2. Don't worry if you tend to get nervous and flustered. This may only worry and employer if the job involves constant decision-making or possible confrontation. Otherwise a skilled interviewer makes allowances for natural nervousness.

3. Before the interview, read up as much as you can about the employing organization, and note the details of the job for which you are applying. Make notes on anything that is not clear, and ask about it at the end of the interview. Also, watch the local newspaper to see if there is any news of the organization.

4. Remind yourself before the interview of what you put in your CV, so that you don't contradict yourself.

5. Take along any extra material which might interest the employer (things you have written, or project material).

6. Dress appropriately for the occasion. This is difficult and depends on the job, but good rules are (a) err on the side of formality (when in doubt) and (b) wear what makes you feel comfortable and relaxed.

7. Be on time. Aim to arrive early, so that you are not out of breath, and have time to go to the loo and have a cup of coffee!

Looking ahead – applying for jobs

Make sure you have the employer's telephone number so that you can phone and apologize if you bus or train is late, or your car breaks down. If you *are* late, apologize again when you meet the interviewer.

8. During the interview, try to speak as clearly as possible. If there is more than one interviewer, try to look at everybody in turn. Answer all the questions, but if you don't understand a question, ask them to rephrase it.

If you get the impression that the interview is not going well, don't show your discouragement. You have nothing to lose by appearing confident, and the last few minutes of an interview can sometime change a first impression.

If you are terrified of interviews

Many careers officers at colleges will offer you a trial interview, so do take advantage of that, and have a good discussion afterwards about what was good or bad about your behaviour at the interview.

Go over the whole thing again afterwards, with friends or relations, and ask them to 'put you through your paces' until you learn to answer difficult questions without visible signs of distress. Learn to keep your personal, domestic or financial problems out of the conversations. Work out beforehand what kind of questions you think you will be asked, and how to answer them. For example, you may be asked how you will cope with a full-time job if you have children to look after. This is a delicate area, and you must not show that you feel incensed because the employer would probably not ask this question of a male applicant. Rather than showing your anger, point out firmly that you have made all the necessary arrangements to combine work and childcare (and, if it is the case, indicate that the children's father shares equally the responsibility).

Another difficult question to answer is, "Why are you interested in this particular job?" So think hard about this beforehand. Obviously, you *are* interested, or you would not have applied, but it is not always easy to put your feelings into words. If you anticipate such trouble, ask around before the interview and find someone who would *not* consider doing the job. Ask his/her reasons, and argue in favour of the job; this will give you a clue about why you find the job attractive.

Some other questions you might face are:
"What skills do you think this job requires?"
"What part of the job do you expect to find most difficult?"
"What do you hope to be doing in five years' time?"

A good interviewer will soon get you relaxed and talking. Not all interviewers are good, of course; some are untrained, inexperienced, or incompetent. But most of them are pleasant to deal with. If you come across an interviewer who is deliberately provocative or disagreeable, tell him/her that this is not a well-approved technique and ask to be treated with more courtesy.

Possible snags

You may face discrimination because of your age. Most employers think they know how to treat juniors, but they are often confused about how they would deal with an older woman. In some jobs there are definite age limits on entry, the justification usually being the career ladder, and it being essential for entrants to pass through each career stage by a certain upper age.

Other employers do not have rigid age limits but are biased against older applicants in that they are cautious about taking anyone who has been out of employment for several years. But such an employer might be looking for someone with special skills of the kind you can offer, and would make an exception in your case.

You might face sex discrimination. The 1970s dawned with great hope for British women, with two important Acts in their favour – on Equal Pay and Sex Discrimination – reaching the Statute Book. But the 1980s petered out in a depressing twilight in which women's earnings actually declined as a proportion of men's, and the number of unemployed women increased rapidly. However, all is not doom and gloom for women with skills and education. Generally speaking, at all times (including recessions) graduates and others with job skills enjoy an advantage in the job market.

In a few professions, such as teaching and the Civil Service, equal pay has long been the order of the day (though women seem to get few of the more responsible and higher-paid jobs). On the subject of sex discrimination, it is interesting to see a report in a London University student newspaper in 1982, on a large firm of accountants which was recruiting equal numbers of male and female graduates. A woman partner in the firm said that, when recruiting, she looked for the same qualities in men as in women: the ability to get on with people, a sense of humour, a person who doesn't get fed up in a hurry. She said she found no difference between men and women in approach, commitment or performance. But women seemed less prepared to devote their entire lives to a career, and tended to draw the line at a 75-hour working week. She said high female absenteeism was a myth, however, and that more men than women dropped out altogether from a job with her firm. So it seemed to her that few men *or* women wanted to be 'married to the job'.

As an older woman, you will have to be realistic about your job prospects. Are you willing to take a job anywhere in the country? Would your husband or partner change his job if necessary, to fit in with your plans? Do you need to be near aged parents? Is it impossible for you to move because of your children's education? Men face these difficulties too, of course, but not usually at the stage when they are applying for their first job.

If you restrict the type of work you will do, and the areas you will work in, you will find you have a very narrow choice available.

Think positively

Getting a job is difficult at any stage of your life, and you may feel nervous about competing with younger people. But you've got lots of points in your favour:

- Women live nearly 7 years longer than men, on average. So a woman of 40 has a life expectancy of between 35 and 40 years, during most of which she can be highly productive.

It's never too late ...

- Academic research has shown that, while mathematical ability may decline slightly with age, our conceptual thinking actually improves as we get older.
- Research has shown that some employers actually prefer to employ older women. They reckon they are working because they genuinely want to (although most women *need the money they earn*), and probably will not leave to have more children. Child care is rarely an insoluble problem for older women, because the children are usually at school and are often old enough to take care of themselves during school holidays. And because of family responsibilities of various kinds, an older woman is unlikely to move suddenly.
- Choosing a career is no longer a once-and-for-all decision for *anyone*. The world of work is changing so fast that most people have to retrain for another job at some time in their lives. So taking courses in mid-life or in mid-career is going to be normal for everyone in future.

Using the skills and talents you acquire through education and training, be more willing to come forward and apply for responsible jobs. Have confidence in your abilities and show that you welcome a challenge.

People with skills and education are Britain's greatest asset, and women have not yet shown fully how much they can contribute when they are fully qualified.

Chapter 12
People like you

Now meet some mature women students who took courses of various kinds and won through to change their lives. You will probably find someone whose circumstances are not unlike your own. Nearly all of them started from a position where they had little formal education beyond the minimum school-leaving age. Coming from different backgrounds and lifestyles, they faced different problems. Some of them had unexpected twists in their lives, but all feel they profited from their student experience.

I want to make clear that these women are real people whose names have been changed. My reason for giving case-studies, rather than presenting the results of a controlled survey of mature students' attitudes, is that I am not very interested in 'Mrs Average with 2·4 children': no such woman exists. I don't even think there is such a person as a 'typical mature woman student', though there are some clear similarities between women who are thirsty for learning. In reporting on some mature women students, it is *their* perceptions of what happened to them that are given, and you will doubtless find them interesting.

Note that the women in these case histories returned to education and training in the 1970s, took exams called O levels, which are now known as GCSEs, used TOPS government training schemes which are now known as ETS courses, and often went to polytechnics which are now the new universities.

1. Anne

Name	Anne
Age she started the course	39
Marital status	Married to a garage mechanic.
Children	2, under 15.
Education	Secondary modern school. No qualifications.

It's never too late ...

Work experience	Worked in a shoe factory for 10 years until marriage (factory now closed). At home for 15 years.
Reason for taking course	"To find out whether I was capable of working with people again, and if I had anything to offer."
The course she did	A WOW course at a technical college (full-time for six weeks).

What she got out of it

Anne responded to a newspaper advertisement of the Wider Opportunities for Women (WOW) course. She says it gave her confidence and enthusiasm for seeking jobs, whereas previously she had been feeling very despondent. At the end she had a good idea what to aim for, and saw possibilities for jobs she hadn't previously considered. She enjoyed being part of a group on the course, and realized that she was not the only woman around who didn't know what to do. She also enjoyed hearing other people's backgrounds, opinions on life, and approaches to work, though she says that discussions always seemed to end up in a kitchen sink drama. Information ranging from how to use the Jobcentre to all the courses available from the Training Services Division (TSD) – of which she was previously only vaguely aware – were useful not only for herself but for her friends who want to return to work. Finding out what employers look for in applications and personal interviews had been helpful, as well. Anne thinks the WOW courses should be advertised a lot more, because most women she has spoken to don't know they exist.

What she did when she finished the course

Anne wanted to get a job right away, and she accepted a job in a Salvation Army hostel canteen and loves it. She has got interested in the problems of the people she meets at the hostel, and is going to take an evening class dealing with social problems, so that she will understand them better. She says it was the WOW course that gave her the confidence to join an evening class, too.

The family's response

Anne says she proved to her unbelieving husband that she could

People like you

get up and out of the house before 8.15 a.m. And she had managed almost as usual with the housework and shopping. She was relieved to find that the home and children didn't totally fall apart when she was going out every day. But her husband and the children were having to do more for themselves since she started work full time.

Both Anne and her husband think the investment in the course was well worthwhile.

2. Beryl

Name	Beryl
Age she started the course	29
Marital status	Married to a civil servant (clerical officer).
Children	2 young children, 1 at nursery.
Education	Comprehensive school; left with five O levels at age 16.
Post-school	Full-time secretarial course.
Work experience	Office work until she married. Then at home for eight years.
Reason for taking course	Interested in a cookery course and a teacher's certificate.
The course she did	NOW course at a polytechnic, followed by City and Guilds courses.

What she got out of it
The New Opportunities for Women (NOW) course showed Beryl how few opportunities are open to women unless they take some form of training. She decided to combine her interests in cookery and teaching, and found out from a student counsellor at a local adult education college that this might be possible by taking City and Guilds cookery courses, followed by an FE Teacher's Certificate. The NOW course lasted one day a week for ten weeks, 10 a.m. to 3 p.m., and her younger child attended the college nursery that day. The day was divided into two sessions, one before and one after lunch. In the first hour, students had a series of lectures on relevant aspects of industrial and occupational

sociology, leading to a survey of women's employment. In the second and third hours two guest speakers from a range of occupations came to talk about career opportunities and training in their particular field. In the fourth hour students formed seminar groups and discussed papers on chosen topics. One whole day was set aside for simulated interviews, when a visiting management consultant played the part of interviewer. In the preceding week, students were asked to choose an advertisement for a job, complete a curriculum vitae and be prepared to be interviewed for that post (as a training exercise). The simulated interviews were conducted in front of the class and criticisms and suggestions invited from the audience. Initially the women were apprehensive, Beryl says, but they appreciated how useful the exercise would be when they later went for an actual job interview.

Students could opt to take a battery of tests of ability and interests, lasting four hours, and conducted by psychologists. Most opted to take them and then had an opportunity to discuss their test results individually with the psychologist. Students with personal problems of a domestic or psychological nature were introduced to a counsellor.

The range of occupations covered by speakers was wide, but there were clearly limits to the realistic opportunities for mature women. Professions which have a long training or are in high demand by school leavers imposed high hurdles.

What she did when she finished the course

Beryl took City and Guilds courses in cookery, first at ordinary and then at advanced level, and went on to gain the FE Teacher's Certificate. She then got a job teaching in a college of technology and is delighted.

The family's response

Beryl's husband has helped her a lot, encouraging her to do the courses and sharing the household responsibilities. Taking an interest in his wife's cookery courses, he has become something of a 'cordon bleu' cook himself. Beryl thinks that her studying and career are a 'family affair' and everyone has contributed to making it possible. The course fees were sometimes a strain on the family budget, but were well worth the effort, she feels.

3. Carol

Name	Carol
Age she started course	45
Marital status	Widow
Children	4, all at home.
Education	Grammar school, left at 16 with School Certificate.
Post-school	WEA classes.
Work experience	Employed full-time (clerical) for five years, then at home and doing voluntary work in a pre-school playgroup.
Reason for taking course	Interested in the education of young children, and teaching possibilities.
The course she did	NOW course, followed by TOPS retraining course.

What she got out of it

Carol says she benefited greatly from attending the NOW course (similar in detail to that taken by Beryl, see above), as it was extremely interesting and helpful, stimulating her into looking around seriously for a satisfying job and restoring some of her vanished confidence. It opened up new horizons, but made it abundantly clear, on the other hand, what she was not capable of tackling. She thought the course fee was expensive for her, as a widow, but the college reduced her fee.

Carol took the Government Retraining Scheme (TOPS) Shorthand/Typist course at the local college of further education. Having been told that she would be paid for her training, she was disheartened to receive less than half the full amount of TOPS grant because she was a widow receiving a widow's pension. She enjoyed the course, though.

What she did when she finished the course

She soon afterwards applied for and got the job of school secretary at a large comprehensive school. She feels that she can both earn her living and learn much more about children's education. She keeps up her educational interests by taking WEA classes, and looks after her health by attending keep-fit classes. She is delighted that she made the effort to go to these courses.

The family's response
Since her husband died, some years ago, Carol has had to persuade her children to take a large share of the housework, and consequently there was no great difficulty for her here. Her children were pleased that she was moving out of the home and making new friends, and that she now has a job. The time is shortly coming when her children will begin to leave home, and Carol realizes she needs to be prepared for this change in her life, when for the first time since she was a young girl she will again be a free agent.

4. Dana

Name	Dana
Age she started course	35
Marital status	Married to a plumber.
Children	2 in 9–15 age group.
Education	Grammar school, left at 16 without qualifications.
Work experience	Office work and some first-aid nursing, then at home and doing voluntary work.
Reason for taking course	To obtain O levels and train for a career.
The course she did	NOW course at polytechnic, followed by O level courses at college of adult education.

What she got out of it
The NOW course made her aware that she was not too old to obtain O levels in as many as five subjects and train for an entirely new career. She felt inspired to enrol at a college of adult education, where the tutors were used to dealing with adults' problems of learning, and over a period of 3 years she took five O levels and passed them. She took two O level courses each year

in each of the first two years (part-time day and part-time evening work) and a fifth O level in the third year. She had no criticism of the teaching and help she received on the courses.

What she did when she finished the course
Dana applied for training as a nurse at a big teaching hospital and qualified as an SEN. She is very happy working 32 hours a week on a mixed medical ward, but plans to take a three-month district nursing course. She chose SEN course rather than SRN because the SRN course involved spending a year in another hospital, on a split-shift basis, and she felt this would be too demanding in addition to her family commitments.

The family's response
Dana's husband knew of her interest in nursing and fully backed up her fairly long programme of getting the necessary O levels so that she could train at a hospital. She says he has always helped out with housework and childcare, and is not fussy about how the house looks as long as there is food on the table. She likes to know that the house is clean, even if it is untidy, so the whole family joins in a weekly clean-up.

Dana and her husband think the course fees she paid were very reasonable indeed; she thinks education at local authority colleges is very good value for money. Each course she took cost about £10 per term, but she says costs will have increased a lot.

5. Elaine

Name	Elaine
Age she started course	29
Marital status	Married to a poly lecturer (ex-serviceman).
Children	3, aged between 2 and 7.
Education	Secondary modern. Left at 16 with 3 good O levels.
Work experience	Joined armed services, trained as clerk.
Reason for taking course	Wanted to take a degree, as her husband had done.

It's never too late ...

The course she did   O and A levels followed by a degree course at a university.

What she got out of it
Elaine's husband had left the Army and was taking a degree at a northern university. Elaine was inspired by his example and decided to follow suit, if possible. She decided to get the traditional qualifications for university entrance, and enrolled at a local college of education, taking two O levels in the first year, and two A levels at the end of a further two-year course. She didn't greatly enjoy the courses, which she thought were a grind, and she said the teachers had no idea of the special problems of older students. But she found that her husband could help her a lot, since he was also studying. Her husband took a postgraduate teaching course at the university, so that he was just completing his education when Elaine was ready to begin hers. When he was studying for finals, Elaine felt responsible for all the housework and childcare, but she took evening classes so that her husband could do the baby-sitting. When Elaine became a full-time history student (at the same university and indeed in the same department) her husband Brian accepted that it was his turn to take responsibility for housework and major childcare. He got various teaching jobs in schools and FD colleges, and eventually got a lectureship at a polytechnic.

Elaine greatly enjoyed being a mature student at university. She met a number of other older students and they formed a network to help each other and meet socially. She was active in campus politics. Since she got a grant in her own right (not a full grant, but substantial because her husband's earnings were not high) from the local education authority, the family's finances were reasonable during her period of study, though they were struggling to buy a house.

She took a good upper-second class degree and went on to do a postgraduate teaching course.

What she did when she finished the course
Elaine was fortunate to get a teaching post right away. She had greatly impressed one of the schools where she had done teaching practice, and when a vacancy arose there she applied

People like you

and got the job. It is a large comprehensive school. Elaine finds the work exhausting but thoroughly satisfying.

The family's response
Elaine speaks highly of her husband's help and support throughout her course. He was able to help her with housework, childcare and with her studies, which cemented their personal relationship. Their children showed signs from time to time of resenting the way both parents, one after the other, were involved in student life, but at these times Elaine and Brian devoted extra time to them, and took them up to the university to join in sports activities, so that they felt part of the university campus too.

6. Gillian

Name	Gillian
Age she started course	40
Marital status	Married to builder.
Children	4, aged between 6 and 16.
Education	Grammar school, nine O and 3 A levels. Left school at 18.
Post-school	Trained nurse (SRN) and midwife. One-year course for health visitors.
Work experience	Hospitals, then district nurse.
Reason for taking course	Developed multiple sclerosis and could not continue nursing; was looking for alternative career.
The course she did	Full-time degree course at nearby university.

What she got out of it
Gillian wanted to write and lecture on the care of babies and young children, but she also wanted to keep as many options open as possible. Taking advice from a friend who was a mature student, she chose to study psychology (particularly child psychology), educational research and linguistics at a university which allowed multiple subjects. She was determined that her lecturers and tutors should not know about her disability, which

was not then affecting her noticeably, though she had definite problems. She wanted to be treated exactly like other students. But she never knew when her right hand (her writing hand) would cease temporarily to function, so she needed an understanding friend to take lecture notes in duplicate (using ordinary carbon paper) from time to time. Examinations were obviously going to pose problems, too, but fortunately she found that she had the option of taking three of her courses as projects, and could also take three other courses which would be marked entirely by continuous assessment methods (so no written exams). This meant that at her finals she wrote only three examinations of the traditional kind, which was a great relief. Tiredness was her main problem, because she cannot stand for long periods. As far as household jobs are concerned, she has learned to do them sitting down (ironing, peeling vegetables and so on). She gave up practically all her hobbies, and entertaining of friends, and she had no energy for social life at the university.

Academically, Gillian had few problems. Having taken the course for health visitors at a polytechnic some years earlier, she knew she could handle the assignment and essay writing. As far as relations with her teachers were concerned, she thought they had little sympathy for older students. As for her own handicap, she now thinks it would have been wiser to make continual references to it, instead of struggling to play it down, because her teachers never seemed to remember that she had special difficulties unless she reminded them. Despite this, however, she succeeded, and got a very good degree.

What she did when she finished the course
She was shortlisted for a lecturing job with the Open University. Although she did not get it, she was delighted to get as far as an interview. She is now lecturing at the local college of further education, teaching nurses, and also wants to do some postgraduate research. The multiple sclerosis is getting worse, and she does not make long-term plans, living each day as it comes and enjoying what is good about it.

The family's response
Her husband had a good income, and was totally supportive of her wish to do the degree course. He and the children were used

to sharing the household tasks, because Gillian had worked full-time for some years already, and the family could also afford to pay for help with the housework. They bought a dishwasher, and made the children entirely responsible for stacking and unstacking it. Her husband took over all the shopping in her final year as a student, and throughout the course did as much cooking as Gillian did. Every Saturday he took the children out for the day, leaving her to get on with her project work. Gillian remains the organizer of the household, however, seeing it as her job to do this.

7. Hanne

Name	Hanne
Age she started course	48
Marital status	Single.
Children	None.
Education	Boarding school until age 18; School Certificate and Higher School Certificate.
Post-school	Secretarial training, nursing training.
Work experience	Secretary to doctors; took nursing training and worked in a hospital; then fund raising for Spastics Society; then assisting experimental psychologist.
Reason for taking course	Realized that lack of formal qualifications was hindering her career.
The course she did	Degree course at a polytechnic.

What she got out of it
Hanne first applied to a London polytechnic to take a one-year diploma course in social work. In the final group interview for one of the 20 places (200 applicants were involved), she was redirected to an interview with tutors in social work and psychology, and they advised her that it would be more appropriate for her to take a degree course. Hanne, the daughter of wealthy and cultured Austrian parents, had been

It's never too late ...

sent to England as a child refugee.

She had no difficulty in getting a full grant from the local education authority, not having had any grant previously and not having taken any course of higher education before. But it was clearly fortuitous that she landed up on a full-time degree course.

Hanne took a B.A. in Social Sciences. This was a compendium of Social Policy, Social Administration, History, Politics, Economics, Psychology, Sociology and Law. The degree was awarded on the basis of continuous assessment, plus end-of-year examinations, final examination in five subjects, plus a thesis on a subject chosen by herself, with subsequent viva voce (a sort of cross-examination). Her thesis was based on 9 months' regular casework with a family in an area of inner urban deprivation, and examined what help was available from the state or voluntary bodies for such a family.

Hanne enjoyed every bit of the course, except for the maths. She had considerable difficulties in the early stages of her course when advanced standards of maths were expected. Believing she was totally innumerate, Hanne almost gave up the course in the first few weeks. Her young male tutor told her she hadn't a hope in that subject. But she was firmly rescued by the tutor in charge of statistics – a woman of her own age who succeeded, after several coaching lessons, in making Hanne grasp the essentials. She subsequently shed her phobia about maths and got good marks in several economics modules. She thinks the woman tutor was particularly interested in helping women overcome their lack of confidence about maths, and that she was very lucky to meet her.

What she did when she finished the course
Hanne was offered a place on an M.Sc. course in the Sociology of Medicine, but did not take it up because grants for postgraduate work were no longer available, and she needed a job. She says she wishes she had taken a university course, not because she thinks she would have enjoyed it better, but because she thinks there is still a stigma against poly degrees; she thinks this is totally unjustified, but does exist.

Hanne got a job, part-time at first but now full-time, as a student counsellor at a polytechnic. She also got interested in marriage counselling, and has taken a course in marriage guidance. She says she is learning all the time, and is trying to start a self-help group for divorced and separated women. She feels that taking a degree certainly started her on a worthwhile career.

8. Iris

Name	Iris
Age she started course	33
Marital status	Married to railway engineer, later divorced.
Children	4, aged 3 to 10.
Education	Comprehensive school, left at age 16 with six O levels.
Post-school	Shorthand/typing course.
Work experience	Shorthand/typist for 6 years, stayed at home when she had children.
Reason for taking course	Dissatisfied with prospect of a life filled with home and childcare.
The course she did	Open University degree.

What she got out of it

Iris took six years of study to earn an honours degree. She says it was very hard work studying alone as an OU student, but she never had any real difficulty with the academic side of it, and enjoyed greatly the contacts with other students, and the Summer Schools. Her relationship with her husband did not founder as a result of becoming a student: she says she took the course as an escape from a relationship she did not wish to continue, and become wholly wrapped up in her studies. Her husband also developed other interests, and they grew steadily apart; after 15 years of marriage, and part way through the OU course, they were amicably divorced on grounds that the marriage had broken down irretrievably. Iris was awarded custody of the children.

She got consistently high marks for her OU work, and it was no surprise to anyone when she was awarded first class honours.

What she did when she finished the course

She applied for, and obtained, a post as a university lecturer. She

It's never too late ...

pursues a highly successful career, all the more remarkable because few women of any age, experience or type of degree get academic posts in Britain. She feels lucky to have a fairly well-paid job in a profession where equal pay has long been established.

The family's response
Iris says her problems would have been greater if her husband had not been so cooperative both about the divorce and in taking the children for regular visits. He has also never defaulted on payments for his children, and he willingly paid her OU fees.

With four young children to look after, Iris did not have an easy life as a student; she says she is not houseproud, and the children have had to fend for themselves quite a bit, but they have always been well and happy, and as they got older it was easier.

9. Jane

Name	Jane
Age she started course	35
Marital status	Married to a salesman.
Children	5, aged 3 to 12.
Education	Private school to age 18, obtained O and A levels.
Post-school	Secretarial course.
Work experience	Secretary to company director for 5 years.
Reason for taking course	Did not enjoy being a full-time mother and needed an identity of her own.
The course she did	Dip.HE, and then a B.Ed at a college of higher education.

What she got out of it.
Jane chose her course after discussing her plans with a Careers Adviser. She thoroughly enjoyed getting out of her 'domestic bondage', as she described it. Since they were not short of money, they paid for extensive help in the house, and fees for the youngest child to go to a private nursery school. Jane had a car

of her own, so transport to and from college (25 miles away) was easy. She enjoyed the freedom of doing a Dip.HE course, knowing that if she didn't want to go on to do a degree she would probably earn the diploma. However, she did decide to take the degree, including a teaching qualification, and found the work relatively easy.

What she did when she finished the course
What had interested her friends was that Jane chose a teaching qualification, which seems so close to the role of a parent. But when she came out of college, there were no teaching jobs available in the area where she lived, and she could not travel far because of her family commitments. For the moment she is happy to be qualified, and free to apply for any jobs that come up. Alternatively, she is toying with the idea of starting a private nursery school, using her training in that way.

The family's response
Jane's husband, John, was totally baffled by her wish for an education and a career outside the home. By his creed, wives did not work unless they were obliged to, and this was a reflection on the husband as provider. But when he realized that Jane was not by nature a born mother (though she was a very caring person) and that she was beginning to resent having so many children, he saw that she needed outside interests and supported her in her college studies. Jane thinks he was a bit scared that she might walk out on them all one day, if she continued to be so depressed, and he saw college work as an outlet for her pent-up emotions.

As far as the children are concerned, they now say they realized when they were young that their mother did not enjoy being with small children all the time, and that life became more relaxed for them after she went to college.

10. Karen

Name	Karen
Age she started course	42
Marital status	Separated (husband a teacher).

It's never too late ...

Children	2, aged 9 and 14.
Education	Secondary modern school to age 15, left without qualifications.
Work experience	Shop assistant until she had children, then at home. Occasional part-time work in shops.
Reason for taking course	Needed training for a better job when her husband left her.
The course she did	Open University foundation course. Then business studies course at a poly.

What she got out of it

Karen was deeply shocked when her husband left her to live with someone else. He could not afford much by way of maintenance payments, so she needed a reasonably paid job. She went to work in a shop for a time and having read out the OU in a newspaper, enrolled for an Open University foundation course, to see if she could cope with academic work. She did well at this, but realized she would be better off as a full-time student on a course for which she got an automatic grant. On the strength of the OU foundation course she was admitted to a business studies degree course at a poly about 20 miles away, so she was able to travel daily to college. Life on a grant was not easy, but on the other hand there were some subsidized activities for students, and she got quite a lot of extra financial help from local authorities, in the form of free school meals and uniform allowance for the children, and rent and rate rebates.

One of the things she most enjoyed about the course was being sent off to do periods of work with local employers. At one of these firms they were so impressed by her enthusiasm and energy that they offered her a permanent job when she got her degree. Her only criticism of the course was that, if she had not already had a lot of help from the OU in return-to-study skills, she would have been very much out of her depth in the first year.

What she did when she finished the course

She accepted the job with the local firm, and is happily looking after the export side of an engineering works, using her up-to-date knowledge of business methods and the commercial French she studied.

The family's response

She says her son, who was 14 when her husband left, was a tower of strength in supporting her, and looking after the younger boy when she had late classes, or could not be at home for half-term school holidays. The younger boy was very upset by his father leaving, but her husband had kept in constant touch and often took the boys out for a whole day at the weekends.

Karen is very thankful that opportunities for education and training were available, at no cost to herself when she became a full-time student. Without these, she thinks she would have remained a very bitter person, and not been able to survive so well.

Conclusion

These are just a few examples of women who have gone back to education in later life and have succeeded. As you can see, they are people like you. And there are thousands more. If you can't recognize yourself in any of the above case-studies, be assured there were many different women students who were interviewed, from the wealthy landowner's wife who was bored with showing tourists round her country house, to the abandoned common-law wife with four children living on social security. They had all won through to emotional and economic independence, and one, over-enthusiastic, went as far as to declare, "Education is a thrilling as sex, and it lasts longer!"

Unlike material goods, education can be shared without being diminished. The more knowledge and understanding you have of the world around you, the more you have to share with your partner, your children, your family and your friends. It is not a question of showing off what you know, but of having the imaginative sympathy to put yourself in other people's shoes and see things from their point of view. So 'going back to school' will not only make you more skilled and confident, but more understanding of others and therefore nicer to know.

If, after reading this book, you feel that becoming a mature student is not for you, then at least it will have saved you the hassle of finding out the hard way. But if you have 'caught the bug' and want to go on learning, then remember that it is never too late to

- go to college
- learn a new skill
- make up for lost opportunities in education.

Other titles in Impact Practical Guides series

The Complete Book of Child Safety

Cohen, Kilham & Oates
in association with the Child Accident
Prevention Trust

ISBN 1 874687 17 X £5.95

Be Your Child's Natural Teacher

Geraldine Taylor

ISBN 1 874687 10 2 £6.95

Planting Acorns
How to give your city child a country childhood

Geraldine Taylor

ISBN 0 245 54389 9 £7.95

Impact Reference series

Visitor's UK
An A to Z user manual to the UK

Brian Slack

ISBN 1 874687 18 8 £7.95

Curious Customs
*A guide to local customs and festivals
throughout the British Isles*

Martin Green

ISBN 1 874687 19 6 £4.95

French Glossary for Bilingual Secretaries
French-English/English-French

ISBN 1 874687 23 4 £6.95

French Glossary of Information Technology
French-English/English-French

ISBN 1 874687 24 2 £6.95

French Glossary of Commercial Terms
French-English/English-French

ISBN 1 874687 25 0 £6.95

French Glossary of Accountancy and Management
French-English/English-French

ISBN 1 874687 26 9 £6.95